Franz Delitzsch, William Clifton Daland

Solemn Questions Addressed to Hebrews of Culture

Franz Delitzsch, William Clifton Daland

Solemn Questions Addressed to Hebrews of Culture

ISBN/EAN: 9783337316099

Printed in Europe, USA, Canada, Australia, Japan

Cover: Foto ©Suzi / pixelio.de

More available books at **www.hansebooks.com**

Solemn Questions

ADDRESSED TO

Hebrews of Culture.

BY

PROF. FRANZ DELITZSCH.

Translated from the German

by the

Rev. WILLIAM C. DALAND.

Alfred Centre, N. Y.:
The American Sabbath Tract Society.

Solemn Questions

ADDRESSED TO

Hebrews of Culture.

BY

PROF. FRANZ DELITZSCH.

Translated from the German

by the

Rev. *WILLIAM C. DALAND.*

Alfred Centre, N. Y.:
The American Sabbath Tract Society.
1890.

PREFACE.

No apology is necessary for presenting to the public an English translation of this most excellent of tracts. Already but about two years before the world in the German language, it has won the respectful attention of both Jewish and Christian thinkers everywhere, and has proven itself to be the best text-book for Jewish catechumens. This translation appeared in volume II. of *The Peculiar People*, and it is now issued as a separate pamphlet in the hope that thereby in this newer garb it may continue its gracious work among the English speaking Jews.

That God, who has so lately removed from us the lamented author, may vouchsafe His blessing upon Israel and raise up for His chosen people many friends, to whom the life of Franz Delitzsch may be an inspiration to noble endeavor in this cause, is the earnest prayer of

THE TRANSLATOR.

No apology is necessary for presenting...

Solemn Questions

ADDRESSED TO HEBREWS OF CULTURE.

Beloved Hebrew Readers,—If, as I hope, you know me as a Christian scholar who is a friend of Israel, you will understand that in inviting you to a religious meditation, I am anxious to put myself in your place and realize your mode of thinking. I shall take nothing for granted except that upon which we are both agreed, and offer you only cogent reasons capable of producing irresistible conviction.

There is a God. Such is your belief as well as mine. We are bound to believe it. In vain do atheists and epicureans strive to escape from it. It is of the essential nature of our spirit to trace every effect to some cause, and as we climb this ladder of conclusions higher and higher, we arrive at last at a being who is the cause of all causes, the last cause of the universe, a being independent of everything, and on whom everything is dependent, a being to whom everything which exists owes its origin. The universe without God is but a blind monster. History without God is nothing but confusion, without · rhyme or reason. And there is but one God. Two or three highest beings side by side are impossible; one only can be the highest. But this one God, on whom man depends in every breath, and whose glory the heavens declare, wants to be acknowledged and praised to the exclusion of all else. Among all the truths to which our reason must yield, there is none higher than this, that God is one; and among all the duties incumbent upon creatures endowed with reason, there is none higher than this, that they give glory to the One God only.

I admit to you, my dear Jewish readers, frankly, that the Christian religion would be a false religion if it gave up or tampered with the belief that God is one. In that

case, the Jewish religion would have comparatively a
stronger claim than the Christian religion to ascribe to
tself the destiny of becoming the universal religion. For
our chief weapon against heathenism is the declaration
that the gods of the heathen are but deified creatures, and
that the true, living God is One, even the Creator of heaven
and earth. Neither am I inclined to withhold from you
the admission that Christian worship, sometimes, by its
ceremonies and prayers seems to contradict the confession
of faith in one God.

The Reformation has done away with some of the
abuses and errors which bear the stamp of heathenism,
because they curtail the glory of the one God. The Reformation has laid down the principle, that the doctrine and
practice of the church is ever liable to the test of the words
of Scripture. The creeds of the Reformers, designate the
holy books of the Old and New Testaments as "the pure
sources of Israel," to which the church must ever have re-
course to formulate by them its doctrine and to regulate by
them its life. The Israel of the Old Testament, too, has to
judge of the merits of the New Testament religion by the
documents of that religion, and *the church has not the right to
force upon Israel the Christian religion in this or that historical
garb.*

On the other hand, the Israelite who wishes to have a
true conception of the Christian faith, is bound not to be
guided by accidental impressions or second-hand hear-say,
but to search for what Jesus and his apostles affirm. He
will then find that the fundamental principle of the unity
of God, which proves the incomparable superiority of the
religion of Israel over all religions of antiquity, is, in the
New Testament, too, acknowledged as the supreme truth.
When one of the scribes, as related in Mark 12: 28, 29,
asked Jesus, "Which is the first commandment of all?"
He answered: "The first of all the commandments is: "Hear,
O Israel, the Lord our God is one Lord." And in Luke 18:
18, 19 we read: "A certain ruler asked him, saying: Good
Master, What shall I do to inherit eternal life?" to which
the answer of Jesus was: "Why callest thou me good?

None is good save *one, that is, God.*" And in the prayer he offers to his Father before his crucifixion, he says, (John 17: 3), "And this is life eternal, that they might know thee *the only true God*, and Jesus Christ whom thou hast sent." And like an echo of this word of Jesus is what Paul writes in 1 Cor. 8: 6, " To us there is but *one God*, the Father, of whom are all things, and we in him, and one Lord Jesus Christ, by whom are all things, and we by him." Such declarations concerning the *only one God* run through the whole New Testament. " But," it will be objected, "you believe in God as triune." Certainly, but if the "trinity " excluded the "unity," we would give up the trinity and stand by the unity. ·

We believe in God, and in God's Son, and in God's Holy Spirit, just as you believe in God, and in his " Shechinah " and in his Holy Spirit. The essence of God is one, but threefold is the revelation of that essence. Even in the sacred history of the Old Testament he gives a threefold revelation of himself. But, for the present, we will not further touch upon that.   ·

For our further discussion I shall take nothing for granted except that we are agreed on the existence of God. and on the unity of God.

―――――

If God is the creator of the world, He is also its preserver and governor. And if man is free to give to his actions this or that direction, he is also morally responsible. Both those things are self-evident. And since there are free beings in the world, the history of the world cannot follow the same laws as govern the material universe. There is a law in the natural world, and there is a moral order in history in accordance with a higher law. The attitude of men towards God is determining the attitude of God towards men. And because men, in their estrangement from God and in the misery of sin, cannot save themselves, God, who is not only just but, before all things, merciful and gracious, interposes and provides means of salvation for man, and substitutes mercy for justice in the case of all who do not reject His proffered help.

Such a means of salvation was the call of Abraham away from his idolatrous surroundings to make him prophet of the one living God for his house and all the world. "Get thee out of thy country and from thy kindred, and from thy father's house, unto a land that I will show thee. And I will make of thee a great nation, and I will bless thee, and make thy name great, and thou shalt be a blessing." Gen. 12 : 1, 2. In these divine words Abraham is called to become a channel of blessing, a fountain from which far-reaching streams of blessings are to flow. Whether people participate in the blessing conveyed through Abraham or not depends upon the attitude they assume towards him, as stated in the third verse of the chapter cited above, "And I will bless them that bless thee, and curse him that curseth thee: and in thee shall all families of the earth be blessed." Such was God's will, design, and promise which came through Abraham, upon Isaac, Jacob and the people descended from them.

The patriarchs were not without sinful weaknesses, and the people of Israel had a natural inclination towards heathenism, as is evident by their repeated yielding to the fasination of the idolatrous worship of their neighbors. But in so far as Israel and their ancestors proved themselves true servants and preachers of the one living God, and of His counsel and will, in so far has God, who shapes history according to his plan of salvation, demanded that His human instruments be obediently acknowledged by those who came under their influence as having a divine mission.

The patriarchal form of revealed religion was followed by the Law of Moses, and this latter by the Messianic revelation. When Jesus was baptized by John in Jordan, and again when He was transfigured upon the mountain, "there came a voice out of the cloud saying: This is my beloved Son, hear him." Luke 9: 35. This divine witness declares him to be the Prophet like unto Moses, concerning whom we read the solemn words of warning exhortation: "And it shall come to pass that whosoever will not hearken unto my words which he shall speak in my name, I will require it of him." Deut. 18: 19. It declares Him to be the

Servant of Jehovah of whom God, in the word of prophecy, says, "Behold my servant, whom I uphold, mine elect in whom my soul delighteth; I have put my spirit upon him; he shall bring forth judgment to the Gentiles " (Isaiah 42: 1); *i. e.*, it is He whom God has appointed that through Him the religion of Israel shall become the religion of the world. He is the " Son " of whom it is said in the second Psalm: " Kiss the Son lest He (the Lord God) be angry, and ye perish from the way." For as we read in John 3: 35, 36, " The Father loveth the Son, and hath given all things into his hand. He that believeth on the Son hath everlasting life; and he that believeth not the Son, shall not see life, but the wrath of God abideth on him." And He himself in His sermon on the Mount demands faith, living faith, confession of the heart and life, for on that day He will say to all who only outwardly subject themselves to Him, " I never knew you; depart from me, ye that work iniquity." Matt. 7: 23.

These are mighty words, which even a Jewish hearer ought not to leave unheeded. May not this Jesus be, after all, the man whom God has appointed as the instrument to *complete* the channel of salvation begun by Abraham and continued by Moses? Of the success which Abraham's proclamation of the one true God had beyond the limits of his own household, we do not read anything; on the contrary, in Egypt and Philistia he himself made all success impossible by his unfaithful conduct. Neither have Moses and the people of Israel done anything to convert the heathen world from its dead idols to the living God. Even among the prophets there is but one, namely, Jonah, who was sent to the great Empire-city to preach repentance there, and he did it only reluctantly, yielding to a divine compulsion. But apostolic preaching emanating from Jesus has destroyed the heathenism of the Roman Empire, so that Julian the Apostate tried in vain to resuscitate it. True, the mission of the Christian religion in later centuries has not come up in its effect to the first centuries, in which the first impulse given by Jesus himself was more strongly felt. True, the Christian religion has, by admit-

ting all kinds of strange errors, weakened its own original
energy. Yet even the later centuries have had successes
in the heathen world to which nothing that Judaism has
done can be compared. And whenever the Christian religion has found entrance it has permeated the intellectual,
social and political life with power and progress, and has
created a new era in the world's history.

But in the Talmud this Jesus is reviled as a bastard,[1]
the son of criminal intercourse between a certain Pandera
with the virgin Mary, and we are told that He was with
Joshua Ben Perachia (who, however, lived a century before
Jesus) in Egypt, and that He there so misconducted Himself that He was solemnly excommunicated. His miracles
are explained as a consequence of his having hidden, in an
incision in his flesh, certain formulas of witchcraft obtained
in Egypt. Instead of the twelve apostles five disciples are
enumerated, and to each one a name is given indicating
his deserving to be cut off. Jesus Himself, we are told, was
hung at Lydda as a seducer of the people, and is deservedly
suffering greater punishment than Balaam, seeing that He
—it is terrible to have to write it—is being sodden in a lake
of [2] ——— —— ——. Do not reply that you have never read
anything like it in the Talmud. The censor of former days
has struck out such passages. But there are books in which
those condemned passages "like jewels and pearls" are
collected and reserved from oblivion.

Must there not be something rotten in the Talmudical
Judaism which harbors such a hatred against Jesus? May
it not be true concerning Jesus as concerning Abraham,
"I will bless them that bless thee, and curse him that
curseth thee?" Those revilings read like the insane rav-
ings of those who had drunk of the cup of the divine
wrath.

Neither, I pray you, reply that this contempt for the
person of Jesus is owing to His having called Himself the
Son of God and to His having assumed a relationship towards God which is incompatible with the unity of God.

1) ממזר   2) נדון בציאה רותחת

For at all events, there remains His moral purity, His spiritual grandeur, His world-renewing power, before which the greatest modern thinkers bow down, their free-thinking propensities notwithstanding. "I consider the Gospels"—Goethe said on the 11th of March, 1832—"thoroughly genuine, for there is active in them a reflex of nobility which emanated from the power of Jesus, and is of as divine a nature as has ever been experienced on earth. If I am asked whether my nature allows me to adore Him with reverence, I answer: Most certainly! I bow before Him as the highest revelation of the loftiest principle of morality." And Carlyle—certainly not a Christian in the strict ecclesiastical sense—says somewhere: "If you ask me up to what height has humanity reached in religion, I say, look upon our Divine symbol, Jesus of Nazareth, and His life and His biography. Higher than that human mind has never risen."

There are in Israel, too, noble individuals who speak approximately in the same strain. In the writings of Leopold Kompert and Karl Emil Franzos we come across beautiful acknowledgements of the pure and holy humanity of Jesus, though they do not draw the conclusion that the Christian religion is a higher religious platform than Judaism. We are glad even of this approach to right appreciation. He who does not curse him is close to blessing Him and to being blessed by the God whose " Shechinah " He is.

THE time is past, or ought to be past, when hatred of the Jews looked upon every one of the Jewish nation as having had part in the putting to death of Jesus, and thought to do service to God, if it inflicted upon them condign punishment for that awful deed. It has been forgotten that at the time of the crucifixion there were Jewish communities in all three continents who knew nothing of the activity of Jesus in Palestine, nor of his death. But, on the other hand, it is as vain to try to deny or to minimize the guilt of the Jews in reference to the crucifixion. Thus, Philippson, in his pamphlet "Have the Jews crucified Jesus?" tries to whitewash the Jews in the same way in which the tribunals of the inquisition ascribed the murder of the heretics they had condemned to death to the action of the civil power.   And Graetz, after having described, as he thinks with the impartiality of an·historian, the person and work of Jesus, says when coming to the crucifixion: "Such was the end of the man who had worked for the moral improvement of his people and had perhaps become the victim of a misunderstanding." Perhaps! That is to say, the saying of Jesus in which He called Himself the Son of God was perhaps understood in a sense different from what was involved.   But we are of the opinion that the proceedings at the condemnation of Jesus were indeed up-roarious, that the laws were not minutely observed, and that the appeal to Pilate: " If thou let this man go, thou art not Cæsar's friend; whosoever maketh himself a king speaketh against Cæsar " (John 19: 12) was a piece of deceit practiced upon the cowardice of the procurator.   But apart from this, we admit that this Jesus, who in His sermon on the Mount went so far as to criticise even the Decalogue and to oppose to it His own words, saying: " But I say unto you," who called Himself not only the Son of God but Lord of the Sabbath, and declared such rabbinical ordinances as washing of hands before meals as worthless,—we admit I say, that this Jesus could not but appear, from this point of view of Pharisaic legality, as guilty of death; for trans-gression of legal ordinances designed to protect the Law from being broken is, according to traditional maxims a capital offense (Erubin 21 b), and such a teacher was to be executed at the time of the feast. (Sanhedrin 11, 4).   But still the killing of Jesus was, when looked at from a higher point of view, judicial murder.   The justice which carried out the letter of the law was a crying injustice.   For the absolutely perfect purity of the person of Jesus, the over whelming spiritual power of His declarations, and the miracles of mercy in which God owned and acknowledged Him, ought to have lifted His opponents above the platform of rigorous legality. This legality, in nailing the Holy One of God to the cross, has pronounced judgment against it-self.   Just as Paul, who, before his conversion, consenting to the stoning of Stephen, proceeded against the disciples of our Lord with threatenings and slaughter, learned by his own doings of what criminal cruelty Pharisaic fanaticism is capable; and just as he says in Gal. 2: 19, " I through the law am dead to the law "—just so the religion of the law, in delivering up to death on the cross the Founder of the New Covenant promised by the prophet, has borne testimony to its own miserable erroneous narrowness and sealed its own downfall.

We are far from considering every individual Israelite of later times living out of Palestine as responsible for the legal proceedings on that decisive occasion. But, considering that if any people, through common origin, common religion, ceremonial law and history is a compact unity, it is the Jewish people, according to the proverb: "All are responsible for one another,"[1] we cannot escape from the conclusion that the delivering up of Jesus to the Romans as one guilty of a capital offense is a national guilt resting upon the Jewish people; and when we read in the prophet that Israel in the latter days will smite his breast in repentance, and will lament as a fearful crime the killing of a servant of the Lord who had been shamefully misjudged, we cannot escape the question of our conscience whether, after all, Jesus was not the victim of this unfortunate blindness.

"I will pour upon the house of David"—we read in the Book of Zechariah, 12: 10—13: 1— "and upon the inhabitants of Jerusalem, the spirit of grace and of supplications, and they shall look upon me whom they have pierced, and they shall mourn for him, as one mourneth for his only son, and shall be in bitterness for him, as one that is in bitterness for his first-born. In that day shall there be a great mourning in Jerusalem, as the mourning of Hadadrimmon in the valley of Megiddon. And the land shall mourn, every family apart; the family of the house of David apart, and their wives apart; the family of the house of Nathan apart, and their wives apart;

---

1) כורי עיבים זה בזה

the family of the house of Levi apart, and their
wives apart; the family of Shimei apart, and their wives
apart. All the families that remain, every family apart,
and their wives apart. In that day there shall be a fountain opened to the house of David, and to the inhabitants
of Jerusalem for sin and for uncleanness." It is a national
mourning as was once that for the beloved king Josiah
who had been mortally wounded on the battle field of Megiddon. The royal house in its principal branch, as well
as in its lateral branches (David, Nathan); the priestly
family, in its principal branches and its lateral
branches, (Levi, Shimei)—all will mourn, and not
only they but all families existing at that future
time of Israel's great repentance. The special em-
phasis laid upon the mourning of the women shows
that the prophet does not speak of a mere national political
concern, but that he describes a matter affecting man's
relationship to God wherein duties and rights belong to
men and women alike. But who is this Pierced One whose
piercing the Lord God considers as a crime committed
against Himself?

"Whom they have pierced"—it might be thought that
not His own people, but the heathen are described as those
who pierced Him. But in the book of the Prophet Isaiah
we learn that the innocent Servant of the Lord was persecuted by His own people for whom He sacrificed Himself.
"I gave my back to the smiters, and my cheeks to them
that plucked off the hair; I hid not my face from shame
and spitting." Isa. 50: 6.

He came unto His own, and His own received Him not.
And yet the time is to come in which they would recognize as their Saviour Him whom they had misjudged,
hated with a deadly hatred, and persecuted. "Surely, he
hath borne our griefs, and carried our sorrows: yet we did
esteem him stricken, smitten of God, and afflicted. But
he was wounded for our transgressions, he was bruised for
our iniquities: the chastisement of our peace was upon
him; and with his stripes we are healed." Isa. 53 : 4, 5.

Who is this pierced one? Surely not Israel! For

Israel, as a nation, confesses here that he had deemed Him smitten of God who for Israel's sake had taken upon Himself suffering unto death, just as Job had been deemed by his three friends to be an exceptionally great sinner because of his abnormally great trials. If the Servant of the Lord who has been misjudged by His people is the personification of a multitude, He can personify only those who have labored for the salvation of their people and sacrificed their lives to that labor. Such a servant of the Lord was Jeremiah, who, according to trustworthy reports, suffered martyrdom in Egypt at the hands of its people. But this Jeremiah, or any other like him, was only a type of that incomparably great Sufferer, who was consumed by His zeal for the house of God, and who interceded for His benighted people when he gave up the ghost on the cross. When Pilate wanted to release Him, but was hindered by force, the fanatical multitude took all the responsibility upon itself, crying: "His blood be on us and on our children." Matt. 27 : 25. Is it, after all, this blood-guiltiness which will be felt by the Jewish people hereafter as a burden upon heart and conscience too heavy to bear—is that, after all, the national sin for which, when it once comes to the faith, it will ask and receive forgiveness?

One of the last words of Jesus addressed to His people as He was concluding His public activity was: "O Jerusalem, Jerusalem, thou that killest the prophets, and stonest them which are sent unto thee, how often would I have gathered thy children together, even as a hen gathereth her chickens under her wings, and ye would not!. Behold, your house is left unto you desolate. For I say unto you, Ye shall not see me henceforth, till ye shall say. Blessed is he that cometh in the name of the Lord." Matt. 23 : 37-39. Brethren of the house of Israel, you know the view of your ancestors : "The curse of a wise man, even though unjustly pronounced, is effectual."[1] (Berachoth 56 a.) This is an extravagant idea, for an unjustifiable curse, though pronounced by the greatest scholar, is vain

---

1) קללת חכם אפילו בחנם היא באה.

breath. But that a threat out of the mouth of a man living in God and speaking out of communion with God is not without effect has been confirmed by experience. And seeing that that threat of Jesus was followed, four decades after, by the burning of the Temple and dissolution of the Jewish commonwealth, does there not seem to be a connection between the threat and the occurrence of the threatened disaster?

In the "Sayings of the Fathers" (*Aboth.* 5, 9), among the chief sins causing "Galuth," *i. e.*, expulsion from the native country, is enumerated the "shedding of blood."[1] The innocent blood with which king Manasseh filled Jerusalem, from end to end, filled up the measure of sin for which the exile to Babylon was the punishment. But that exile lasted only, in round numbers, 70 years, whilst now the Jewish people has, for 1800 years, been deprived of its country. Yet that country which since the time of Vespasian and Titus has been under foreign dominion has been promised, yea sworn, to Israel as an eternal possession. How is that to be explained? Only two reasons are possible. Either that promise which runs through all parts of the Old Testament, belongs to the region of mythical accounts, or the conduct of Israel, these 1800 years, has made it impossible for God to re-instate them in the promised possession. The prophets have forseen this long expatriation. When those who have been dispersed in all directions recognize the cause and repent, they shall, according to Deut. 30: 1-8, have restored to them the land of their inheritance.

But are not the prayers of the Synagogue—especially those of New Year, Day of Atonement and the intervening days,[2]) full of deep acknowledgement of sin and touching appeals to the mercy of God?

Yes, it is true; but the duration of these many centuries of exile is inexplicable without the assumption that there rests upon this poor people, in spite of its heart-rending

---

1) שְׁפִיכוּת דָמִים.
2) יָמִים נוֹרָאִים.

cries to God, the ban of unacknowledged sin which hin-
ders God from relieving its misery.

HE who accepts the Christian religion as the continua-
tion and consummation of Israel's religion will find this
view amply affirmed in the Law, the Prophets and the
Hagiographa. But these confirmations are no proofs for
the outsider; and in putting questions to the conscience of
the Jewish reader, I pass by all pleas which are without
cogency for him who has not yet accepted the Christian
faith. I will base my arguments upon suppositions which
are accepted both by the believing Israelite and the believing Christian, and chiefly upon these two assumptions:
firstly, that there is a history of God's revelation, *i. e.*, of
God's free acts and communications by which he has interrupted the natural course of things; and, secondly, that
prophecy is an effect of divine revelation, not being the
result of natural combination, but having proceeded from
divine illumination.

If there is no history of divine revelation, Anti-semitism is right in asserting that Israel's consciousness of being the chosen people of God, destined to communicate to
the world God's revelation, is nothing but the vanity of a
conceited national pride. And if there is no prophecy
resting upon the inspiration of the Spirit of God, all the
facts in which the Christian religion recognizes the fulfillment of Old Testament prophecies, as, for instance, that
the good Shepherd in the book of Zechariah was given by
the ungrateful people as His price, thirty pieces of silver,
and that thirty pieces of silver, the reward of betrayal on
the part of Judas Iscariot, are the mere play of chance.
The Israelite who adopts such a position rejects the Christian religion at the cost of depriving his own religion of
its divine basis—he is a "denier of the first cause,"[1] un-
dermining and cutting up the divine root of the Jewish
and Christian religion alike.

But supposing that we, my Jewish reader and myself,

---

1) כופר בעקר.

are agreed in recognizing the hand of God in history and prophecy, I shall carefully avoid what has often been done, namely, to make use of passages in the Prophets, the explanation of which is of a disputable character. I shall not adduce Gen. 49:10 as proof that Shiloh (the Messiah,) is to come at a time when Judah shall have lost the regal dominion. I consider this explanation wrong, and the fulfillment, supposing the explanation could be admitted, would not be correct, for Jesus appeared in the time of the dominion of the Herodean dynasty. That dynasty was, indeed, of Edomitic origin, but, according to religious profession, it was Jewish. According to *Sota*, 41 a, when King Agrippa wept in reading Deut. 17:15, "One from among thy brethren shalt thou set king over thee," the people tried to comfort him by shouting, "You *are* our brother!"[1] and indeed he was their brother, the Edomites having been, two hundred years before, by circumcision, incorporated into the Jewish nation when the Hasmonean king, John Hyrcanus, conquered them. Still less is it possible to prove from the seventy weeks in the 9th chapter of the book of Daniel, that Jesus is the Messiah, because after He had been removed, and Jerusalem afterward destroyed, seven and sixty-two weeks, *i. e.*, sixty-nine times seven years had elapsed. In the first instance "Messiah"[2] may be the legal title of the high priest, who was violently removed, and secondly, the backward calculation of four hundred and eighty-three years brings us to no event of real importance which might serve as a starting point.

Daniel's seventy weeks are an enigma which awaits yet its solution, because it has been found that Antiochus Epiphanes was not yet the final arch-enemy of the people of God, and after his removal it was not yet the final redemption which was brought about, but only a prelude to it.

Prophetic foresight of the distant future is subject to the law of perspective. The end appears side by side with the immediate future, but when the latter is reached there appears between it and the end an expanse of time. What

---

1) אחינן אתה אחינן אתה.   2) משיח.

in the perspective seemed shrunk together is now widely
extended. The prophets of the time of the exile connected
with the end of the captivity, and the faithful believers in
the time of the Selucidæ connected with the end of the tyr-
anny of Antiochus Epiphanes extraordinary hopes, which,
when these respective consummations occurred, were only
imperfectly fulfilled. This is by no means derogatory to
the value of prophecy; it is simply God's order that the
look into the distant, and the look into the immediate future—the divine and the human—should be combined in it.

In one point the prophets of the time of the exile are
agreed; they knew only two temples, that of Solomon, the
first house,[1] which the Chaldæans destroyed, and a post-exilic
temple, the *second house*.[2] The temple described by Ezekiel
is not a third temple of stone which is to be erected at the
end of time, when the second temple shall have met with
the same fate as the first (a fate nowhere foretold), but it
is an ideal for the realization of which the post-exilic
prophet hoped, when Israel shall have repented (Ezek. 43:
10, 11), and all his tribes, and with renewed first love returned to the land of their fathers, a condition which was
not fulfilled. Chapters 40 to 48, of the book of Ezekiel, are
an unfulfilled prophecy. On account of their disagreement
with the pre-exilic and post-exilic order of divine service,
they are for the synagogue an unsolved riddle, so that their
explanation is a task reserved for Elijah.[3] On their account
the whole book of Ezekiel was in danger of being declared
apocryphal; but a certain Chanania, with a store of three
hundred barrels of oil, retired to his study and happily explained away all the contradictions against the Law. (*Chagiga*, 13 a.) Such is the assertion, but nowhere do we find
samples of their supposed reconciliation, nor does this temple anywhere appear as the goal of Israel's hope. In fact,
there is no such thing as a *third* temple mentioned by Ezekiel; there is a second temple, as it was to be according to
Ezekiel's conception, but it was never really built.

When by permission of Cyrus, a number of exiles under

---

1) בית ראשׁין.   2) בית שׁני.

3) פרשה זו עתיד אליהו לדרשה.

Zerubbabel, the prince, and Joshua, the high priest, had
returned to their fatherland, the foundation of a new temple was laid, in 534 B. C., the second year after the return.
The building was soon interrupted, but was resumed in 520
B. C., the second year of the reign of Darius Hystaspes. In
this year, the second of the reign of Darius, was it that
Haggai and Zechariah began to preach. These both proph-
esy that the beginning of the Messianic time would occur
in the time of this temple. " The glory of this latter house,"
we read in Haggai 2: 9, " shall be greater than of the former, saith the Lord of hosts; and in this place will I give
peace, saith the Lord of hosts."

And in Zechariah 3: 8, we read: " Hear now, O Joshua,
the high priest, thou, and thy fellows that sit with thee,
for they are men wondered at: for, behold, I will bring
forth my servant, THE BRANCH." From the time that Isaiah
4: 2, Jeremiah 23: 5, and 33: 15, were written, THE BRANCH
had been the name of the Messiah, as of the branch of
David which was to grow from lowliness to glory, and to
spread around him everywhere salvation and glory.

In the 6th chapter of Zechariah we read that the prophet
was to make " crowns and set them upon the head of Joshua, the son of Josedech, the high priest," that he may represent in a picture what was to come: " Behold the man
whose name is THE BRANCH, and he shall grow up out of
his place (his home), and he shall build the temple of the
Lord; and he shall bear the glory, and shall sit and rule
upon his throne; and he shall be a priest upon his throne;
and the counsel of peace shall be between them both (viz.,
the high priest and the king, *i. e.*, the two offices now separated from one another)."

At the time when this prophecy was spoken the building of the second temple had been resumed by permission
of Darius. It was easy to see that it would be far behind
the Solomonic temple in magnificence. But it is endowed
with all the more glorious promises. It is to be the abode of
peace; the Prince of Peace, king and priest in one person,
after the order of Melchizedek, is to appear in the time of
this temple. In the sixth year of Darius, in 506 B. C., the

building was finished. Under these circumstances, the temple which THE BRANCH builds, the Son of David, the ultimate fulfillment of the promise given in 2 Samuel 7, can be no *third* temple of stone. History moves forward, not backward. But what *kind* of temple was he to build? If Jesus is the Messiah, we have an intimation regarding it in the answer He gives after having cast out of the temple the money-changers and those that sold sacrificial animals, to those who wanted to know what authority He had for His actions. That answer was an enigma even to His disciples. "Destroy this temple and in three days I will raise it up." John 2: 19. Here, too, the temple which was to come in place of the post-exilic temple restored by Herod, is certainly not one of stone.

Supposing the temple which THE BRANCH was to build was to be one of stone, we should have to assume the appearance of THE BRANCH to occur at a time when the second temple is destroyed. But that would contradict Malachi, the last of the three post-exilic prophets, who prophesies in the 1st verse of his 3d chapter: "Behold, I will send my messenger, and he shall prepare the way before me; and the Lord, whom ye seek, shall suddenly come to his temple, even the messenger of the covenant whom ye delight in; behold, he shall come, saith the Lord of hosts."

Here are three different persons introduced. The way-preparing messenger, viz., Elijah, as he is called later on; the Lord, *i. e.*, God; and the Messenger of the Covenant, *i. e.*, the Mediator of the new covenant promised by the prophets. Jer. 31:31, Isa. 42:6; 49:8. What we are to understand is, I suppose, that the coming of this Mediator of this covenant is, indirectly, the coming Lord Himself. But what we are concerned with is only this: that the day of the Lord, which accomplishes judgment and salvation, and ushers in the time of the new covenant, occurs during the time of the second temple. This second temple has, however, been more than fifteen hundred years removed from the holy mountain, so that not one stone has remained upon another.

Has, after all, that been fulfilled long ago, which you,

my dear Jewish reader, expect yet to come hereafter? Is
not, after all, perhaps, that Jesus who once addressed to
the Jewish people the words, "Behold, your house is left
unto you desolate,"—is not He, after all, THE BRANCH[1] spok-
en of by Zechariah, and "*the Messenger of the Covenant*"[2]
spoken of by Malachi? Has He not truly ushered in a new
time in which the kingdom of God went over from the
rightful basis to the other nations, as Malachi, according
to the 1st chapter and 11th verse, declares to have actually
seen? These are questions addressed to the conscience,
which every Israelite to whom truth is dearer than his ac-
customed notions, should ask himself, as in the sight of God.

———

IT is then, a spiritual temple of living stones, which,
according to the prospect held out by Zechariah's prophecy,
THE BRANCH, who combines in himself the priestly and royal offices, would build. The congregation of the New Covenant, whose mediator is the messenger predicted by Malachi, is this spiritual temple. For it is a congregation,
gathered, in the first instance, out of Israel, but afterwards
breaking down the national limitation, and reaching out
towards all nations. It is a congregation, not kept together
by the bonds of consanguinity, but it is a spiritual congregation, united by their unity with the God of revelation.
The Old Covenant is dissolved after it has been shown to be
insufficient to realize the counsel of God which is directed
toward the whole race of man. National privilege has
ceased after having performed its preparatory service.
The law of Israel is a national law, and as such is unsuit-
able to become the rule of life for a congregation composed
of all nations. It was a preparatory step, and is now, since
Christ appeared, an obsolete platform. The Prophets, and
Psalmists, and the writers of the so-called Books of Wis-
dom,[3] laid, already, stress upon the essential in religion;
they deprecated the external compliance with ceremonial
laws, demanded in place of animal and vegetable sacrifices
self-dedication of the inner man, and reduced the real will

———

1) צמח.   2) מלאך הברית.   3) ספרי הכמה.

of God, whose reflex are the ceremonial prescriptions, to
the real and immediate religious concerns. They prepared
for what has been realized by the Christian religion, namely, the deepening and widening of the religion of the Law.
Of course, if the Mosaic law were truly an unchangeable
divine revelation, Judaism would be right in opposing the
Christian religion. Maimonides takes up that position;
but not without opposition from other Jewish dogmatists
like Isaac Albo, who maintains: God Himself may, in
changed circumstances, declare a change in what He originally commanded. A proof of this is to be found, *e. g.*, in
the relationship of the laws given in the book of Deuteronomy, dating from the fortieth year after the exodus, toward the law given from Sinai in the first year.

That the Hebrew male slave should be free in the seventh year, according to Ex. 21: 2, is, according to Deut. 15:
12, extended into granting the same privilege to the Hebrew
maid-servant. The general law, in Ex. 21: 16, that the
stealing of men is to be punished with death, is narrowed,
according to Deut. 24: 7, so as to apply only to the case of the
stolen person who has been sold as a slave, being a Hebrew.
While, according to Lev. 17: 3, no sacrificial animal may be
slain except at the tabernacle, the killing of animals for do-
mestic use is, according to Deut. 12, allowed in any locality.
And again, the old law, according to which, wherever God
is present, a plain altar of earth, or uncut stones, and without steps, should be erected, according to Ex. 20: 24 ff, was
superseded by the erection of the tabernacle and the brazen
altar,[1] and by the demand of the book of Deuteronomy for
a central sanctuary, as the exclusive place for sacrifices.
These are only a few examples, which might be augmented
by others referring to laws about festivals as given in the
Pentateuch. The names of the festivals, the number of the
great feasts, the prescriptions referring to sacrifices,—all
have been modified, in the course of time. And if, within
the time covered by the Pentateuch, the law underwent
changes, why should changes which have a right to lay

1) מִזְבַּח הַנְּחוּשֶׁת.

claim to divine authority, be considered impossible in the time after the Pentateuch? The prophets prove the contrary. The law, according to Deut. 23: 2, excludes all eunuchs from the congregation of the Lord. But the prophet Isaiah, according to 56: 3-5, of his book, breaks through this barrier of the law, and comforts the eunuchs returning from Babylon by the promise of membership with all its rights. It might be objected that though such modifications in isolated cases might be admissible, the complete abrogation of the ceremonial law is inconceivable.

But for the prophets there exists no such insurmountable difficulty. "Wherewith shall I come before the Lord," we read in Micah 6: 6-8, "and bow myself before the high God? Shall I come before him with burnt offerings, with calves of a year old? Will the Lord be pleased with thousands of rams, or with ten thousands of rivers of oil? Shall I give my first-born for my transgression, the fruit of my body for the sin of my soul? He hath showed thee, O man, what is good; and what doth the Lord require of thee, but to do justly, and to love mercy, and to walk humbly with thy God?"

And Jeremiah says, in deprecation of the hypocritical sacrificial services: "I spake not unto your fathers, nor commanded them in the day that I brought them out of the land of Egypt, concerning burnt-offerings or sacrifices; but this thing commanded I them, saying: Obey my voice, and I will be your God, and ye shall be my people." Jer. 7: 22. These are declarations which sound like anticipations of the future abrogation of the ceremonial law.

It is different, indeed, with Ezekiel, who, in chapters 40 to 48, propounds a new ceremonial law for the whole of Israel returned from the land of exile. But the new ecclesiastical and political commonwealth which he describes has not been realized, its conditions having remained unfulfilled. But this part of the book of Ezekiel is on this very ground an important part of the canon of the Scriptures, that it furnishes a clear proof against the immutability of the Mosaic law.

The Midrash says frequently that the Holy One—bless-

ed be He—will give a new law through the Messiah. The
new feature of this law is that it discloses the object and
spirit of the old.

Does not the preacher of the Sermon on the Mount
correspond to this picture of the future?

And another passage in the Midrash says: In the days
of the Messiah all sacrifices will cease, except thank-offer-
ings.[1] Is not Jesus, perhaps, after all, that servant of the
Lord who, according to the prophecy in Isa. 53: 10, will
" make his soul an offering for sin,"[2] for his people?

———

JEWS who are familiar with the New Testament, in
arguing for the immutability of the law, will perhaps appeal to the sayings of Jesus in the Sermon on the Mount
(Matt. 5:17), "Think not that I am come to destroy the
law or the prophets; I am not come to destroy, but to fulfill."
This is the saying which is also cited in the Talmud (tract
Sabbath, 116 b), but incorrectly rendered: "I have not come
to beat down[3] the law of Moses, but to add[4] to it." The
right idea is still to be recognized even in this disfigure-
ment of the meaning of the expression. Far from desiring
to do any injury to the revealed law, or to deny its divine
authority, Jesus—in opposition to an observance of the
law which clung to the letter and considered its external
fulfillment to suffice,—wished to teach and render possible
a deep and true inward realization of the law, which should
comprehend its radical and fundamental principle as the
veritable will and intention of God. As Jesus is the fulfiller of prophecy, since His person and His work is the
realization of what was foretold by the prophets, so also is
He the fulfiller of the law, since as a mediator in word and
deed He has accomplished the realization of what God, the
Law-giver, had in view.

Because He carries the external and ceremonial precepts of the law back to their heart and spirit, it cannot be
drawn from His words that they are to be broken down.

———

(1) היץ מקרבן התורה.   (2) אשם.
(3) למיפהת.   (4) לאוכפי.

On the contrary, He recognizes the binding character of
the whole law at that time, when He adds, in verse 19,
"Whosoever therefore shall break one of these least commandments, and shall teach men so, he shall be called the
least in the kingdom of heaven; but whosoever shall do
and teach them, the same shall be called great in the kingdom of heaven." The kingdom of heaven is identical with
the Messianic kingdom. It is the new order in the universe
and in human life, which has its center and its head in
Jesus Christ. This kingdom of heaven does not come into
existence by means of a sudden breaking down of the old
order, and whoever of his own will looses one of the least
precepts of the revealed law does it at his peril.

Jesus could not speak otherwise during His life and
work here below; for, as Paul wrote to the Galatians (Gal.
4: 4), "When the fullness of the time was come, God sent
forth His Son, made of a woman, made under the law." He
was the bodily son of a Jewish mother, the legal though
not the bodily son of a Jewish father, and through circumcision He was united with the congregation of Israel and
received into participation of its rights and duties. He
defends those of His disciples who set aside the rabbinical
ordinances in regard to the washing of the hands before
meals (Mark 7: 6, 7); He speaks in their behalf when they
plucked ears of corn on the Sabbath in order to appease
their hunger (Mark 2: 23–28); and claims for Himself freedom to do works of benevolence and mercy also upon the
Sabbath; but never do we read that He declared the Sabbath commandment, or any commandment of the Mosaic
law, not to be binding, or that He ever did aught against
the word, the thought, and the spirit of that law. His ad-
herence to the law is, of course, not that of the Pharisees,
but that of the Prophets. When he says, " Not that which
goeth into the mouth defileth a man, but that which cometh out of the mouth, this defileth a man (Matt. 15: 11),
He releases neither Himself nor His disciples from the observance of the dietary laws: but He wishes, nevertheless,
to say that the polluting effect of forbidden food is as nothing in comparison with the polluting effect of foul talk, and

profane, indecent speech. It is similar to the words of the prophet Isaiah, when he says that it is not a fast acceptable to God for a man to afflict his soul and to spread sackcloth and ashes under him, but rather to deal his bread to the hungry, and to bring the poor that are cast out to his house. Isa. 58: 5, 7. And when Jesus said to the Pharisees who complained of His intercourse with publicans and sinners: "Go ye and learn what that meaneth, I will have mercy and not sacrifice." (Matt. 9:13), He simply confirms an old expression of the prophet Hosea (6:6), which He employs as His own. He does not remove the obligation to bring the offerings prescribed for particular cases; for He said to the leper, "Go thy way, show thyself to the priest, and offer the gift that Moses commanded" (Matt. 8:4), and He obliges the one who has quarreled with his brother to interrupt the offering of his gift until he has become reconciled. Matt. 5: 23, 24. He considers, therefore, the offering of the gift to be of service, but He delares that the outward gift is worthless before God if it is not accompanied by the giving up of the evil and hateful self-will. He was one of that people for whom sacrifices were offered in the temple every morning and evening, and on all festivals. He, however, did not feel obliged to bring an offering for Himself personally, for He knew Himself to be without sin, and it is also nowhere related that He appeared before God with a personal offering (the so-called *chagiga*), upon the occasion of the three great feasts according to the old law. Ex. 23: 14–16; 34: 23. The temple tribute of a half-shekel He, however, paid, in order not to give offense, although He felt conscious that He was free from the obligation of the tax of the temple because of His relation of Sonship to the Lord of the temple (Matt. 17:24–27), but He was not able to present an offering for Himself; for His inmost thought was, "Sacrifice and offering thou didst not desire; mine ears hast thou opened; burnt-offering and sin-offering hast thou not required. Then said I, Lo, I come; in the volume of the book it is written of me, I delight to do thy will, O my God; yea, thy law is within my heart." Psa. 40: 7–9, English Bible, 6–8.

He was made under the law, under the law in every
particular, bound by its ceremonies and its statutes in reference to matters of outward life; for so it was God's decree
that He Himself, having submitted to the law, should redeem His people from the constraint and the limitations
and the curse of the law. He was made under the law,
but at the same time He continued the work of the prophets. since He had set those precepts of the law, which had
been observed in the letter by hard and unsanctified hearts,
over against moral duties to man as man, and gave to these
a deeper significance. The law was to wear itself out in
Him, and was to pronounce His death sentence, since zeal
on account of the law persecuted Him even to His death.
It was a boastful Pharisaic strictness as to the letter of
the law which condemned His insistence upon the spirit
of the law as apostasy from the law, and which allowed
itself to rush onward to the blasphemy of the Holy Ghost,
who spoke and worked through Him. And is it not also
true to day, that Reformed Judaism, which opposes itself
to the law from the prophetic stand-point of spiritual great-
ness and moral purity. is willing to recognize the noble
struggle of Jesus, while the so-called orthodox Judaism,
when it is obliged to mention Him, thrusts Him far off
with the imprecation, "May His name and memory be
blotted out?"[1]

He was made under the law until death; but after
He, through His death, entered the life of glory, He was
taken from the limitation of the national law, as also from
attachment to an especial nation. The Thorah, which
was revealed from Him, the exalted Son of God and man,
by means of the Spirit of Pentecost, which followed the
Passover of His death and resurrection, is that law intended for all mankind, concerning which it was prophesied by
Micah and Isaiah, "Out of Zion [as before from Sinai,]
shall go forth the law, and the word of the Lord from
Jerusalem" (Micah 4: 2, Isa. 2: 3), and for which "the isles"
(*i. e.*, the distant heathen lands), "shall wait." Isa. 42: 4.

---

1) ימה שמו וזכרו.

" The law," says Paul, "was our schoolmaster to bring us unto Christ, that we might be justified by faith. But after that faith is come we are no longer under a schoolmaster. ' Gal. 3: 24, 25. The apostle did not live till August, A. D. 70, when the will of God that the national law should yield to the universal law, for which the former was a preparation, was confirmed by the fiery judgment decreed for the temple in Jerusalem. Since then a great part of the ceremonial law has been without force. Numberless commands, which were obligatory in the Holy Land, or in the Temple, could not therefore be put into execution. All the laws of sacrifice, the centre of the ceremonial law, became relaxed; for the legal place of sacrifice lay in ashes, and Zion, the temple mountain, was no longer an Israelitish possession. And this condition of things has lasted, not merely for decades, as at the time of the Babylonian captivity, but for nearly two millenniums; and it seems as though it would last forever. And then, too, the universal feeling brought about by Christianity has effectually destroyed the bloody sacrifice for the Jewish consciousness. Holdheim, the renowned founder of Reformed Judaism, says in his discourse upon the *Ceremonial Law in the Messianic Kingdom*, 1845, p. 40, " We cannot speak of a sacrifice in the Messianic kingdom, since even to-day it is in the highest degree contrary to every pure idea of faith." He sees a confirmation of this in the fact that orthodox Judaism has failed in every attempt to provide for the possibility of sacrifices, although it maintains that the ancient holiness remains to the temple, even in its condition of destruction;[1] we need therefore only to find a piece of the temple court in order to put the law of sacrifice again in operation. But no Rothschild, no Montefiore, no Cremieux, has ever made a single attempt with this in view, for no person in the present state of culture wishes the restoration of a sanctuary which echoes with the groans of dying beasts, and whose floor, like that of a slaughter-house, swims in blood. Religion, spiritualized by Christianity, cannot endure it;

---

1) אע''פ שחרב בקר ושתי עימד.

nor can the Jewish religion escape the influence of this
tendency toward refinement, even though it endeavors to
resist Christianity.

We believe we have here shown that the downfall of
the national ceremonial law, although it could not have
been proclaimed by Jesus Himself, nevertheless, from inward necessity and by a divine decree, was the consequence
of His coming.

THE Christian who believes in the Bible does not yield
to the Israelite in his esteem for the Pentateuchal Law.
He recognizes the revealed character of this law and its
incomparable superiority to all the codes of antiquity. It
maintains its pre-eminent character, as over against the
idea of justice current in Christian states in times past, for
example, in regard to punishment; for it knows no tor-
ture, and it excludes from the death execution those fearful abuses and torments which have characterized even the
penal code of Charles V. And as to civil matters it is pre-
eminent, since by a suitable distribution of the soil it
checked poverty, and by the assurance of hereditary pos-
sessions it prevented the impoverishment of a family.
With justice could Moses, the great law-giver, say, " What
nation is there so great, that hath statutes and judgments
so righteous as all this law, which I set before you this
day?" Deut. 4: 8. And with justice also does David confess in the 19th Psalm, " The law of the Lord is perfect."[1]
The law is really perfect as to its innermost motives and
its ultimate ends. But with equal justice must we con-
cede, as children of the Christian dispensation, that according to the letter it is only relatively perfect. It is very true
that the double command, " Thou shalt love the Lord thy
God with all thine heart, and with all thy soul, and with
all thy might;" (Deut. 6: 5) and, " Thou shalt love thy
neighbor as thyself;"[2] (Lev. 19: 18) expresses the will of
God so completely that even the New Testament revelation can only reiterate these words. Mark 12: 28–34, Rom.
13: 9 ff. But, on the other hand, it is also true that in the

1) ה_תמימה   2) כמוך

context of the Thorah this double command addresses itself to Israel as a nation, as is seen from the fact that the
command to love one's neighbor is especially extended to
the stranger dwelling within the bounds of Israel. Lev. 19:
34. This two-fold command, which binds together the
first and second tables of the Decalogue,[1] likewise lays
down a system of statutes, which have in view the restoration of a holy people, whose king is the all-holy One, and
accordingly for the most part having to do with the external relations of life. The establishment of a national people of God was the necessary preparation for the establishment of a universal people of God from all mankind. The
relationship into which God entered with Israel as His chos-
en people was the ground of the future kingdom of God,
comprehending all nations. The realization of the divine
decree which has for its object the salvation of mankind,
came within the limits of a nationality, not that these limits should abide, but that when they had accomplished
their preparatory end they should be removed. Its entrance within the national limits, had, however, as its result,
a contradiction of the moral ideal. The Law, as national,
cannot avoid an external and particular character insepa-
rable from a state and a nation, and the degree of spiritual
and moral culture among the people made necessary certain adaptations, which could be permitted, since the law-
giver did not claim to bring the true will of God to im
mediate and full realization. The Thorah accommodates
itself to certain firmly rooted habits and customs, such as
blood-revenge, slavery, polygamy, and levirate marriages,
since it is satisfied with certain alleviating, limiting and
regulating restrictions upon them, and contains, here and
there, namely, in the permitted grounds for divorce, some
striking defects, since it restricts them to the limits of
what is at present attainable. In comparison with other
legal codes of the ancient world, it amply vindicates its divine origin; but it has also a limited human side, because
of the condition of morality and of culture in its time. It

----

1) עשׂרת הדברים.

conceals an eternal kernel in a temporary shell. Judaism
itself, in the lapse of time, has come to esteem its human
elements as partly impracticable and partly contrary to the
progress of morality.

Polygamy and levirate marriages furnish many in-
structive examples to show that the Mosaic law, as being a
special national code for Israel, is not an expression of the
exact will of God for all mankind equally. These examples also show that the Thorah does not conceal this but
plainly intimates it. Marriage is (Gen. 2: 18 ff) so close a
relation of personal intimacy that it cannot be conceived
except as a relation of two persons only; it is impossible to
think of it as a relation existing at the same time between
one man and several women, or between one woman and
several men. Only monogamy is true marriage; polygamy
contradicts the idea of marriage. Nevertheless, polygamy
is permitted in the Mosaic law. The ancient custom, supported upon the precedent of the patriarchs, was too deeply
rooted to be destroyed. The law with regard to inheritance (Deut. 21:15–17,) shows that a man may have two
proper wives. Another law (Ex. 21:10) assures the right
of one wife against one taken afterward. It is permitted
on certain conditions that one may have as wife or concu-
bine a captive taken in war. Deut. 21:10–14 The law with
regard to the king forbids the king to have many wives,
but without restricting him to monogamy. Deut. 17:17.

The example of David and Solomon shows what re-
sults followed the relaxation of the Thorah in later times.
Jehoiada, the tutor of the young king Joash, took for him
two wives. 2 Chron. 24: 3. And the Thorah even requires
the addition of one wife to another in one case, namely,
in the law of the marriage of brothers-in-law (Deut.25:5 ff)
for the case that the living brother is already married is no
doubt included, although this case, and likewise the case
that the one dead had several wives, is left without mention, and the old custom is not sanctioned, unless possibly
in the *chaliza*, the ceremony described in Deut. 25:9. It in-
dicates a progress in the spirit of the law, if not in con-
formity with its letter, that the Mishna *Jebamoth* extends

the right of chaliza many times casuistically. In the Middle Age. Gerson von Metz (died A. D. 1028), who was called
the Light of the Exiles,[1] forbade polygamy and only permitted it by way of exception, but without being able to
accomplish his end. For almost two centuries the wealthy
French and Spanish Jews lived in bigamy, and it is due to
the increasing influence of Christian government, at least
in Europe, that monogamy became the rule among Jews.
How far the spirit of Christianity struggled against plural
marriages is shown by the secret marriage of the Land-
grave Philip, of Hesse, with Margaret von der Saal, in addition to his marriage with a daughter of George, Duke of
Saxony. This marriage was permitted by both Luther and
Melanchthon. Melanchthon (who was present at the marriage, March 3, 1540,) fell afterwards into a terrible state
of mind on account of this, which brought him to the brink
of the grave. Luther thought afterwards, as well as before,
that he could justify this permission in the sight of God;
but his opinion, that what was permitted in the case of the
patriarchs, might also be permitted to Christians in a case
of extreme necessity, rested upon a narrow view of the
difference between Christianity and the Old Testament
religion.

The rabbi, Dr. Isidor Kalisch (died May 9, 1886. New-
ark, N. J.), one of the most gifted and energetic advocates
of reform, in his *"Ancient and Modern Judaism,"* has put together the beliefs of modern Judaism in ten sections, of
which the third is: "The Mosaic religion is capable of an
endless progress." He means by this its development to a
universal religion. This development is consummated in
the fact that Christanity has come from the bosom of Judaism. Reformed Judaism is Christianity without Christ;
it is a light which denies the source of light from which it
is taken. The seventh section reads: "Traditional ceremonies and customs, whether biblical or not biblical, must
be altered and even abolished as soon as their form vio-
lates the ethics or the feelings of modern civilization."

---

1) מאיר הגולה.

This is a thought which without Christianity could never
find lodgement in a Jewish heart or utterance from a Jewish mouth. Among these customs is polygamy, in regard
to which Christianity antedated Judaism at least a thous-
and years in rejecting it as a matter of principle.

In another point also it is shown that the Mosaic law
is not a direct and complete revelation of God's will. The
law in Deut. 24: 1–4 attempts to check absolute freedom in
divorce, but it declares that the husband has a right to put
away his wife if he finds her in anything shameful.[1] The
extent of the meaning of this leaves room for arbitrariness,
and has caused a multitude of desertions for slight reasons
everywhere where the Jewish people was its own law as to
marriage. Was Jesus not right when He said (Matt. 19:8)
that the law was in this respect far behind the ideal of
marriage, and accommodated itself to the hard hearts of
the people? Is, then, the time yet so far off when Talmudical Judaism shall cease to hate Him, and Reformed Judaism shall begin to give Him honor?

THE ceremonial sacrifices came to an end together with
the ceremonial law. As circumcision was a previously existing custom outside of Israel before it became, by divine
revelation, the covenant sign of the people descending from
Abraham, so also was sacrifice the chief element of Gentile
worship before the Sinaitic law distinctly marked it as the
chief element in the worship of the one true God. With
sacrifice, however, the matter stands quite otherwise than
with circumcision. Circumcision arose from an endeavor
to attain bodily purity, but as a means to this end it was a
custom only among a few nations. But sacrifices are found
among all nations who possess more than an undefined
knowledge of a higher Being. There is a religious necessity which urges man by an inward need to offer sacrifices.
A sacrifice is, according to its fundamental idea, a present
or a gift. It is an offering,[2] as was that of Cain and Abel,

------

1) עָרְוַת דָּבָר.

2) מִנְחָה.

the oldest and first mentioned in the Holy Scriptures. All that man possesses he has from God. He can give nothing to God which was not received from Him before. It is not possible for him to deny himself his whole possession; that would contradict the end for which God gave it. Therefore he gives Him a part, in order by this self-denial to attain the sanctification and blessing of the whole also, though even as a gift the sacrifice has a mediatorial significance. Man lets his sacrifice plead for God's grace in his behalf, just as Jacob sent beforehand an offering[1] to Esau to induce him to be gracious. So man lets his sacrifice step in as a third term between himself and God, that it may work out for him who brings it God's favor and good-will. In this sense a sacrifice is, even now, a way of showing reverence to God. It is a sacrifice to make an altar covering, or a painted window, or any holy vessel for the house of God, or to render it beautiful with flowers.

The matter stands, however, otherwise with the bloody sacrifice, or the offering of slain beasts. That beasts are to be slain in order to afford enjoyment to God, is a crude idea which has place in heathendom, because they have a low conception of divinity. We will, however, on the other hand, leave it uncertain whether in the heathen world the offering of the life of a beast availed as a substitute for the offerer who deemed himself worthy of death. It is enough that there, also, the idea of atonement, or the appeasing of divine anger, is connected with a bloody sacrifice. But the Word of God declares how the blood of the offerings brought to the God of Israel shall be understood; for it is there stated, as a ground for the prohibition of the eating of blood, that "the life of the flesh is in the blood, and I have given it to you upon the altar to make an atonement for your souls; for it is the blood that maketh an atonement for the soul." Lev. 17:11. That the soul is in the blood lies in the nature of the soul and of the blood. But that the blood of beasts is a means of atonement does not follow from the nature of such blood, but from the fact

1) מנחה.

that God has allowed, appointed and ordained it[1] for this
end. It expiates by virtue of the soul (or life) which is in it;
therefore the soul (or life) of the beast comes in as a substitute for the soul of the man, to make an atonement for
it; that is, to shield it from God's anger. We do not wish
to inquire here how we are to regard this substitution, but
this much remains certain, that according to the Sinaitic
law the atonement is connected with blood,[2] that is to that
blood which is brought to the altar, poured out upon it, or
sprinkled on the horns of the altar. All bloody sacrifices,
as such, possess an atoning force. Atonement is not the
chief object of all of them, but always and everywhere
must the application of the blood upon the altar precede
the offering of the sacrifice, in order that this may be received as the gift of one for whom atonement has been made,
that is, of one freed from guilt, and well pleasing to God.

If the matter really stands thus, that for Israel, the
people of the law, the divinely-appointed means of atonement was found in the blood of sacrifices, it may be asked
what means of atonement has taken the place of sacrificial
blood since the destruction of the temple. It is plain that
the reading of the chapter enjoining sacrifice can be no
substitute; the reading of a prescription cannot take the
place of medicine for a sick person. And prayer, repentance, and fasting,[3] could not avail as a substitute, since
prayer, repentance, and self-mortification must be connected with sacrifices, according to their especial object, otherwise they would be but dead works without a corresponding
inward reality; therefore these three could not render
sacrifices superfluous. But one will object—was not the
spiritual worship without temple and sacrifice a matter of
necessity during the seventy years of the Babylonian captivity? Certainly, the people of God should learn by this
period of sojourn in a strange land, that the essence of all
religion is the worship of God in spirit and in truth. The

---

1) נתתיו.

2) אין כפרה אלא בדם.

3) The three ת's; תפלה, prayer, תשובה, repentance, and תענית fasting.

Lord was then to them a "little sanctuary' (Ezek 11:16),
i. e., He took for a time the place of the temple, He shielded
them in communion with Himself as " in his pavilion," " in
the time of trouble." Psa. 27:5. The Exile was a preparatory school to that future in which all sacrifices, except
sacrifices of thanksgiving, shall come to an end.' See *Vay-
yikra rabba*, ch. 9, and elsewhere. But if, after the restoration of sacrificial worship and the second destruction of
the temple, it is now to be thought that the eighteen hundred years which have since passed by, are a repeated
preparation for the Messianic age,—is the conclusion not
to be drawn from the length of this period that the time
has really come for the worship of God in spirit and in
truth, although not recognized by that people for whom
it was especially intended?

In the Prophets and the Psalms the ceremonial offering
is mostly understood as the symbol of a spiritual offering,
principally the offering of one's self, without which and in
comparison with which the ceremonial offering is worthless, *e. g.*, Micah 6:6–8, and Psa. 50. But there is also kept
in view the self-sacrifice of a Servant of God which has a
relation to the ceremonial offerings and to what they accomplish according to God's command, which is that of an.
titype to type. The Servant of God, depicted in Isaiah 52:
13 to 53:12, offers Himself as a sacrifice³ for the sins of His
people. His chastisement accomplishes their peace, and
His wounds bring them healing. He, the Righteous One,
accomplishes a righteousness which proceeds from the sins
for which He makes atonement. And Zechariah, after
prophesying (Zech. 12,) that the Jewish people one day will
look with repentance and longing upon the great Pierced
One, whose piercing the Lord considers as a deed of blood
inflicted upon Himself,⁴ goes on to say : "In that day there
shall be a fountain opened to the house of David and to the

---

1) לְמִקְדָּשׁ מְעָט.
2) לֶעָתִיד לָבֹא כָּל הַקָּרְבָּנוֹת בְּטֵלִין וְקָרְבָּן תּוֹדָה אֵינוּ בָטֵל.
3) אָשָׁם.
4) וְהִבִּיטוּ אֵלִי אֵת אֲשֶׁר דָּקָרוּ

inhabitants of Jerusalem for sin and for uncleanness." Zech
13:1. Therefore, if the people will recognize their offense
against that Pierced One with penitent grief, it will then
be of no avail to doubt that a fountain is opened out of
which flows water which purifies from guilt and impurity·
These are prophetic words of such ·clearness that no one
who connects them with what the gospels relate can silence
his conscience by explaining them away, even by dint of
the most skillful exegesis.

It cannot occur to any one to deny that the great
Pierced One is an individual person. A collective person‐
ality cannot be there meant, but One, namely, Israel's Sav‐
iour, as is evident from Zech. 13:1; for His death, misun‐
derstood as to its basis and purpose, becomes a source of
salvation. But by the Servant of the Lord mentioned in
Isaiah 52:13 to 53:12, many understand a plural number.
The Tenth section of the Confession of Faith constructed
by Isidor Kalisch declares: "Israel's holy calling is to be‐
come the saving Messiah of humanity." But that Servant
of the Lord offers Himself for His people, and that the
whole body of a people should offer themselves for the
whole body of a people is an inconsistency, is a self-contra‐
diction. If the idea of the Servant of the Lord be, never‐
theless, a collective idea, then, in distinction from the mass
of the people, the whole body must be understood of those
who make every effort, and risk everything, in order to
free their people from inward and outward misery, although
misunderstood by them in narrow blindness. But at the
same time it is very natural that in this whole body of the
true servants of the Lord one should tower above others,
and that One should outrank all of them. Should not Jesus
be this incomparable One? Countless Israelites have been
conquered inwardly by this prophetic picture of the future,
for the prophet here depicts the Crucified One[1] as though
He stood under the cross. "That is from the New Testa‐
ment, not from the Old!" cried one, as the 53d chapter of
Isaiah was read to him. And when he was convinced of

1) תהלי.

the contrary he resisted the blinding light, not hesitating to say, " Then Isaiah went too far! "

BUT why do we then need a Mediator?—is the query many a reader will here interject. Everywhere in the Holy Scriptures, whether in the Psalms or elsewhere, when prayer is offered for the forgiveness of sins, the petition is offered directly to the Holy One—Blessed be He!—to Him who has revealed Himself as "tne Lord God, merciful and gracious, long-suffering, and abundant in goodness and truth. keeping mercy for thousands, forgiving iniquity and transgression and sin " (Ex. 34:6, 7); to Him whom praising, the psalmist thus calls upon his own soul, " Bless the Lord, O my soul, and all that is within me bless his holy name. Bless the Lord, O my soul, and forget not all his benefits; who forgiveth all thine iniquities; who healeth all thy diseases; who redeemeth thy life from destruction; who crowneth thee with loving-kindness and tender mercies." Psa. 103: 1–4. On the other hand, we read, " If thou, Lord, shouldst mark iniquities, O Lord, who shall stand?" Psa. 139: 3 But the suppliant knows that God suffers mercy to come upon us instead of justice, and he confirms this when he continues, " But there is forgiveness with thee, that thou mayest be feared " (Psa. 130: 4), that is, " Because thou wilt be honored thankfully, thou forgivest willingly and richly."

Why then do we need a Mediator? In the book of Isaiah we read this saving command, " Let the wicked forsake his way, and the unrighteous man his thoughts, and let him return unto the Lord, and He will have mercy upon him; and to our God, for He will abundantly pardon." Isa. 55:7. But there is even here also the mention of a Mediator, whom the Israel of the future will acknowledge. " The chastisement of our peace was upon him, and with his stripes we are healed." Isa. 53: 5. It will, therefore, be no contradiction that we read in one place, " I, even I, am he that blotteth out thy transgressions for mine own sake " (Isa. 43: 25), and in another place, " By his knowledge shall my righteous servant justfy many; for he shall bear their iniquities." Isa. 55: 11.

Still one will always be able to object that the fifty-third chapter of the book of Isaiah is, nevertheless, isolated, and a doctrine peculiar to the second part of the book of Isaiah can prove nothing against the many other holy books of the Old Testament. Everywhere else it is God Himself who takes away sins and blots them out and covers and forgives them, He alone and for His own sake, of free grace, pure and absolute. We would be treating the evidences for the truth of Christianity too lightly if we ignored the importance of these objections. But the right answer will, at the same time, put in the right light that Christian doctrine which is the especial stone of stumbling for Judaism, the doctrine of the trinity of the Godhead. It is by no means so difficult to understand that God and His Holy Spirit are to be discriminated, and in such a manner, indeed, that the latter is not a blind working force, but an Energy proceeding from God, who dwells in the divine consciousness. But that Christ is God and man in one person, that is what, from the Jewish point of view, is regarded as inconsistent with the unity of God, while it is also by us held to be the fundamental dogma of all true religion.

It is not merely a characteristic of the religion of revelation that in contrast with paganism it consists of the teaching concerning the one God and His attributes in Himself and in relation to His creatures. It is more than that. It is the knowledge obtained through divine witnesses in word and deed, concerning an eternal decree of God to redeem humanity ruined in sin, and concerning the means which He has established in order to accomplish this redemption. Through sin man has become far from God, and God far from man. It is a fundamental postulate of the revealed religion that God, in order to bring back men from their condition of separation from God, and lift them up from the depth of their ruin, must personally, through His own absolute presence, enter into their present human history. In the very first pages of the Bible we read that after the fall of man He personally appeared to him and comforted him in the midst of his condemnation with the

prophecy of victory over the serpent. And the last prophetic voice declares. " The Lord, whom ye seek, shall suddenly come to his temple." Mal. 3: 1. From Obadiah (v. 15)
on, the watchword of all the prophets is, " The day of the
Lord is near," the day in which He will reveal Himself as
Judge and Redeemer in unveiled grandeur. He appears
chiefly as the Redeemer of Israel, for after mankind had
been separated into nations the assurance of the theophany
(divine appearance) received a national coloring.   The
Lord, Israel's God, will come and make Himself known according to His promise. It is the deepest longing of the
people of the old covenant which finds expression in Isaiah
64: 1, " Oh that thou wouldst rend the heavens, that thou
wouldst come down," and the similar expression of hope is
seen in Psa. 50: 3, " Our God shall come." And all creatures
which surround men are called upon (Psa. 96: 11 ff; 98: 7 ff)
to exult with them at the approach of the Coming One.

But if God is to appear historically, and that in such a
manner that He not only talks with one man, as from the
pillar of cloud He talked with Moses at the giving of the
law, but also in such a manner that He comes into an intimate relation with men; then it cannot be otherwise than
that He should make a man the abode of His presence, the
instrument of His thoughts and words, and the fulfiller
of His promise. It could not well be otherwise. And to
this which could not possibly be otherwise the Scripture
witnesses as a reality. As the Angel of the Lord said, " I
am the God of thy father, the God of Abraham, the God
Isaac, and the God of Jacob " (Ex. 3: 6), because the God of
the patriarchs made him the means of attesting His own
presence; so also the Virgin's Son, in whose birth Isaiah
exults, is the bodily presence of the Mighty God, rich in
salvation, and the BRANCH[1] of David is called the " LORD
OUR RIGHTEOUSNESS"[2] (Jer. 23: 6), because, as appears from a comparison with Jer. 33: 16, the Lord, as the
Justifier and Sanctifier of His people dwells in His per-

---

1) צמח.
2) יהוה צדקנו.

son as He dwells in the New Jerusalem. In Zech. 13:7
God calls Him "the man that is my fellow," and this fellowship is so intimate that in Zech. 12:10 He identifies Him
with Himself. The fellowship of God with His prophet is
already so intimate that in the prophetic books the "I" of
God and the "I" of the prophet are exchanged one for the
other; but the fellowship of God with His Messiah, or with
the Servant of the Lord and the Angel of the covenant,
who are prophesied in the books of Isaiah and Malachi,
must be considered as a fellowship still more intimate.
Whether the union of God with Him is capable of dogmat-
ic definition, and how it is to be defined, is here beside our
purpose to discuss.

The words of the dying Jacob, "I have waited for thy
salvation, O Lord" (Gen. 49:18), remain from the beginning to the end of the Old Testament period the unchanged
confession of faith. Salvation is of God, the Lord, who has
established the decree of salvation, and Himself also real-
izes it. Redemption from sin and its consequences, this
radical redemption, over against which every other is but
a fleeting shadow, is everywhere indicated in the Holy
Scriptures as the work of God Himself. That there is a
human mediation in this personal work of God is intimated
in Gen. 3:15, and one cannot think otherwise in view of
this passage; and furthermore, the angels who take part
in the sacred narrative appear in human form and speak
with the human voice. But the acknowledgment of a human mediator, far from being always the same, has its pro-
gressive history. The idea of the Messiah under the figure
of a King, is unsuited to represent the Mediator in a redemption from sin and its consequences. Even in the figure of a King in whom God dwells, the divine King, the
work of the expiation and cleansing of sin is not found;
therefore the incomplete figure of a king becomes enlarged
in the later prophetic writings (Isa. chapters 40 to 66, Zech.
9 to 14, Mal. 3,) to the three-fold figure of the prophetic
declaration of truth, the priestly offering of Himself, and
a more than royal majesty. This future Mediator, who
is Prophet, Priest, and King, in one person, and in whom

the Lord comes to His people (Isa. 50:2), yea, who. according to Mal. 3:1 is the Lord[1] Himself, God calls יְשׁוּעָתִי. Isa 49:6. The joyous message of His coming to the daughter of Zion is in Isa. 62:11, הִנֵּה יִשְׁעֵךְ בָּא. That sounds like: "See, thy Jesus cometh."

This Jesus has said of Himself, "All things are delivered unto me of my Father; and no man knoweth the Son but the Father; neither knoweth any man the Father save the Son, and he to whomsoever the Son will reveal him," Matt. 11:27. With this agrees what he says in John 14:9, 10, "He that hath seen me hath seen the Father," etc. Never did a man dare say such a thing of himself. He is in the Father and the Father in Him; He is the visible representative of God Himself. As a human being He had, as we all have, a temporal beginning; but the Eternal God is so united with Him that our redemption which is wrought · in His sacrificial death, is, nevertheless, the work of God Himself, as Paul says in 2 Cor. 5:19, "God was in Christ reconciling the world unto Himself." This is a mystery into which the angels desire to look, and after the right apprehension of which thoughtful believers have striven since the beginning of the church. When once Israel has recognized in this Jesus the Messiah, then will it assist in promoting a fruitful understanding of this unfathomable mystery.

THE religion of the New Testament contains nothing the foundation of which was not laid as a preparation in the Word of God in the Old Testament. When Paul says of Jesus (Rom. 4:25,) that He was delivered for our offenses and was raised again for our justification, it is essentially the same as what was said of the Servant of the Lord in the 53d chapter of Isaiah. For of Him who, according to God's economy, offered Himself for His people, Israel confesses, as believing in the great wounded Sufferer, "The chastisement of our peace was upon him, and with his stripes we are healed." And even the Lord, who took Him

---

1) הָאָדוֹן.

to Himself from agony and judgment, says of Him who was taken away and lifted up by his persecutors, " By his knowledge shall my righteous Servant justify many, for he shall bear their iniquities." So then, the Servant of the Lord willingly went to his death in order to atone for our sins, and even through death He was exalted of God whose decree He had fulfilled in order to procure for many, *i. e.*, as many as believe on Him, a righteousness which will avail before God, which rests upon the atonement wrought by means of Himself. Christianity does not necessitate to the Israelite new and strange modes of thought, but only this one new thought, that the prophetic word in the Old Testament has come to a full realization in the crucified and risen Jesus.

But how is it to be thought possible that from the voluntary sufferings and death of a man, atonement, justification, and righteousness, accrue to those for whom He takes this suffering and death upon Himself? We will, for the moment, leave it uncertain whether the Servant of the Lord, portrayed in Isaiah 52: 13 to 53: 12 is one person or a plural number; in either case Israel there confesses that salvation and righteousness is wrought for them all through the vicarious suffering and death of One who was long unrecognized, and at last fully acknowledged. How are these to be mentally connected?

Perhaps the following story is not inapt to afford an approach to an insight into the matter. I have it from Hesba Stretton, the English story-writer, who has also written many other stories from which are made manifest the ethical grandeur and moral value of vicarious suffering and death. The scene of the story which I just now recall, is a great London court, in which a countless number of people lived thickly huddled together, for the most part poor and morally degraded. The steward of the house maintained strict government, but he was himself a rough, unbelieving man. A faithful and zealous missionary had for a long time left no means untried in order to bring the light of the gospel to this benighted multitude. His cour-

age and loving tact were exhausted, when his son. a gentle
lad, who was gifted with a lovely voice, offered to go into
the court and to endeavor to touch the hearts of the inhabitants and melt them by striking up some religious songs.
The father knew to what danger his child exposed himself,
but because the salvation of men was to him more than all
else, he yielded at last to the impulse. The boy went day
after day, took his station in the middle of the court, and,
with a voice as clear as a bell, in which his very soul was
felt, began his songs of Jesus. At first there gathered
about him a great crowd, drawn thither by the strange
sight and the enjoyment of the music. But little by little,
as they perceived the intention of his coming, they withdrew, and finally their applause turned to hatred, which
increased to such a pitch that at last the troublesome sing-
er, struck by a stone from the hand of the steward, sank
to the ground and was carried away as one dying. He was
not really so greatly injured as to die, but he was in immi-
nent danger of death, and this danger was enhanced by
his deep sorrow of soul on account of the failure of his
good intention and the rejection of nis kind wish. But
how salutary was the fruit already borne by this sacrifice
of self almost to death! Certainly it did not avail for all
without distinction, but for all those who examined themselves in the presence of this noble young life all but destroyed. The first fruit was this: From the deadly hatred
with which they had requited that love whose wish was to
save them from their depravity, they came to the consciousness of their guilt in all its terrible enormity and worthi-
ness of condemnation. The second fruit was found in this:
That in the bleeding head and pale face of the sufferer
they had before them a picture of innocence able and willing to offer itself a sacrifice for the guilty, an image of divine love which seeks the lost, and a view of that true
righteousness, the essence of which is unselfish love. And
a third fruit was this: That in remorseful self-blame they
cried to God that He might not let the work of this longing, self-sacrificing love, remain unavailing toward them,
and that He would make them partake of the righteous-

ness of this just one against whom they had so grievously
sinned.

And now we ascend from the lower to the higher, from
the comparison to the Incomparable One; from this youth-
ful minstrel whose confession was a note from the many
thousand-voiced choir of believers in every age to that
Servant of the Lord whose very person signifies the salvation of mankind; for the Lord says of Him, "Behold my
servant, whom I uphold; mine elect, in whom my soul delighteth; I have put my Spirit upon him: he shall bring
forth judgment to the Gentiles." Isa. 42: 1. We turn from
this youth, whom sympathy induced to rescue the dwellers
of a neighboring house from their estrangement from God,
to that Servant of the Lord who was decreed to become
the salvation of the world throughout its utmost extent
(Isa. 49: 6), and who accomplished this work as Saviour
with a loving tenderness which would not break the bruised
reed nor quench the smoking flax. Isa. 42: 3. We arise in
thought from this child, whose zealous testimony brought
upon him an illness of perhaps a month, to that Servant of
the Lord, "a man of sorrows and acquainted with grief,"
whose whole life was marked by sympathetic suffering,
and ever full of anguish; from this child whose ardent
love brought him near death, to that Servant of the Lord,
that Pierced and Bruised One who was led as a tender
lamb to the slaughter (Isa. 53: 5-7); from this sick child
around whose couch, conscious of guilt, stand the inmates
of the premises, and even the house steward, to that Servant of the Lord in whose presence an entire great nation
confess their blindness and their sins, through which
they have caused his martyr death. From this we gain an
insight into the moral consequences of the self-sacrifice of
the incomparable Sufferer. In Him it may be seen of what
sin is capable; it outdid itself when it put to death the
Holy One of God as a common malefactor. His death is a
powerful sermon on repentance. In Him it is shown of
what zeal for the law is capable; for it was the people of
the law who, from the stand-point of the law, like the friends
of Job, considered him rejected of God, and in fanatical

devotion to the law, dragged him to the judgment-seat. In Him it is to be seen of what love is capable; for the intensity of His love toward those who hated Him consumed His life, and even when dying He still implored forgiveness for the evil doers. Isa. 53:12. But this love stood in the place of heavenly love, for it was God's will to bruise Him, and it was God Himself who caused Him to sink in such grief.[1] His suffering was the means to a fore-ordained end. His self-sacrifice was to become the ground of His exaltation, and the foundation of a great congregation who should give Him thanks for their redemption and justification. Isa. 53:10, 11. The depth of their iniquity was revealed when they shed the blood of God's Chosen One; and at the same time in that God-ordained, self-sacrificing love there was offered to the sinners a saving hand which brought to those who seized it in faith forgiveness and mercy, and the gracious power to begin a new life. So we see that through the work of the Servant of God, which, suffering, dying, and living again, He accomplishes. there is wroughtf or sinners the knowledge of themselves (repentance), the forgiveness of sins (justification), and a new life, well pleasing to God (righteousness).

"Yes," one will object, "but all that sounds exactly like Christianity." Without doubt it is exactly like Christianity, and yet we have been especially careful not to go outside the thoughts directly or implicitly contained in the 53d chapter of Isaiah. The Messiah, according to an older conception, is a king. But, as in Psa. 110, Zechariah gives to the Branch the priestly crown in addition to his crown as king. And to these two crowns there is added by the second Isaiah and Zechariah the crown of thorns which God transforms into a more than royal crown. The picture of Christ on the easel of prophecy was now ready, and there remained nothing except that the one there portrayed should appear, and that the finger of him who stood as the last of the prophets upon the confines of the two great ages of the world should point to Him and say,·

---

1) ויהיה חפץ דבאי החלי.

"Behold the Lamb of God which taketh away the sin of the world!"

HITHERTO we have drawn our proofs of the fundamental facts and truths of Christianity exclusively from a comparison of them with the Holy Scriptures of the Old Testament. Now we turn our glances toward the Haggada contained in the Talmud and Midrash, the evidential value of which ought not to be underestimated. The strictest followers of the Talmud view the Haggada, in its relation to the Halacha, which fixes the sense of the law, as a purely subjective and fanciful conceit. Yet, nevertheless, even these seize upon the Haggada, whenever it is of value to show that, far higher than the crude and early determination of justice limited to the Jewish nation, there is a humane ethics in accordance with which noble Israelites have at all times acted. For example, in the *Shulchan Aruch* it is stated as an accepted proposition of right and duty for the Israelite to keep the lost property of a Gentile and not to give it back; but the Haggada commends a practice far above this unjust proposition, and relates that the disciples of Simeon ben Shetach bought for their master, who supported himself by flax-combing, an ass, on whose neck they found hanging a pearl. "Now," said they, "thou needest no longer to worry." "But," said he, "doth the owner know of it?" And when they said that he did not, he replied, "Go, then, and restore it to him." *Jer. Mezia, 2: 5.* The Haggada is full of ethical maxims and examples which break through the letter of the written law and the consequences of the traditional law, and touch the spirit of Christianity and its universal and humane morality. Accordingly we read (*Joma 23* a, etc.), "Those who allow themselves to be injured and injure not in return, those who allow themselves to be abused and abuse not in return, who act from love, and rejoice in suffering, of them saith the Scripture, 'Let them that love him be as the sun when he goeth forth in his might.'"[1] Such sayings, which harmonize with the declarations of the primitive Christian rec-

---

1) Judges 5: 31.

ords, are often found in the Talmud and Midrash, and how often have they been offset by mediæval fanaticism and anti-Semitism! Far from lacking evidential force, the Haggada is brought forward even at the present day by the defenders of the Talmud and *Shulchan Aruch*, as a classic witness to save the honor of the nation, and not alone for this end, but also to take away from Christianity and its great universal thoughts their priority, by referring to the religio-ethical maxims, which, like pearls in a jeweler's shop, are scattered partly in the tract *Aboth*, and elsewhere throughout the Talmudic literature. We do not wish here to dispute about this, but we content ourselves with the remark that, with the exception of a very few declarations, all these parallels to the New Testament are later than the first Christian century, and, therefore, if original and independent, they yet follow chronologically.

But they reason unjustly, and employ an inconsistent mode of argument, who, with a proud self-consciousness, exalt those parts of the Talmud and Midrash which harmonize with Christian ethics, and, on the other hand, disparage those portions which agree with the Christian doctrine, as contrary to the spirit of Judaism, and as having come in through yielding to Christian influence. Nathan Krochmal, in his *More Nebuche Hazeman*, who otherwise finds sense and reason throughout the Haggada, condemns these parts as mystical transcendentalism. There is a Hebrew pamphlet entitled נצח ישראל,[1] whose author has cast a superficial glance at Church History, and views these Haggadas as the mire of Christian doctrine deposited in the Talmud and Midrash since the Council of Nice, A. D. 325. Freer from blame is a work on this point by Rabbi Schwartz, in Gablonz, which lies before me in manuscript. It sets out from the proposition that since the Talmudic period there arose within Judaism a two-fold tendency, one mystical and one rationalistic. That is just. The rationalistic tendency viewed a strict observance of the law which justifies and saves, as the principal thing for the present, and

---

[1] The Glory of Israel.

all the future, and allowed to the Prophetic Word almost no influence upon its thought. The Messiah, if it to any extent held fast to a belief in a future Messiah, was, in its view, a king who should adhere to the law and secure for it a universal force. The difference between the present and the Messianic future was considered simply as this, that at some time the שעבוד מלכיות, that is, Israel's servitude beneath the Gentile world-power, would cease. Maimonides, the later representative of this rationalistic tendency, embodied the Messianic conception, rather political than ethical, into his system of Talmudic law. The mystical tendency, on the contrary, hoped in the Messiah a restorer of what was lost through Adam in the fall, a conqueror of the serpent, the mediator of an eternal redemption, and the re-entering of God into human history. Its Messianic idea was not merely an impression from without upon the longing for freedom, but was drawn from the sense of sin and guilt within. It is this conception of the Messiah which floated before Jesus, and upon the realization of which He wasted and sacrificed His life. He did not create it, but only transferred it from an ideal into a reality. Although it does not appear in the Jewish literature just preceding Christianity, and although Jesus' disciples only gradually deepened their external and rationalistic view of the Messiah to this inward mystical and spiritual conception, yet still the Haggada of the Talmud and Midrash prove that it was nothing new and foreign to the Jewish consciousness. Even if not national, it was by no means without foundation; for the Word of God in the Old Testament gave it its characteristic features and color.

In the idyllic picture in the 11th chapter of Isaiah, which corresponds with the close of chapter 65, the prophet says that when the Messianic kingdom shall be set up a new order of things will ensue similar to that in Paradise, before sin came bringing disharmony with the Power governing the world. The Midrash *Bereshith Rabba*, ch. 12, finds this future renewing of the world indicated in the fact that the word *toledhoth* (generations,) occurs but twice in the Bible with a doubled ו, *i. e.*, in Gen. 2:4 and Ruth 4:18.

When these two passages are combined, the opinion is
stated, reasoning from the numerical value of the letter
waw (ו=6), that the doubled ו signifies the six things
which were taken from the first man,[1] and which will, one
day, be restored through the mediation[2] of the Messiah, the
son of David, who is descended from Perez, or, as is expressed by another teacher, "Although all things were created perfect, yet, since the first man fell into sin, they
have come into disorder, and they will not be restored to
their primitive condition till the Son of Perez appears."
Among the six things mentioned above, which were taken
from Adam, is his זיו, i. e., his glorious splendor, his shining
exterior, which was the appearance of his innocence shining forth from his person; for, as is indicated in Judges 5:
31 and Job 14: 20, the love of God makes the countenance
sunny, but God's anger takes away the brightness. All this
agrees with the Christian conception of the work of God in
Christ. It begins within, unseen and spiritual, and its end
and culmination is a new birth ($\pi\alpha\lambda\iota\gamma\gamma\varepsilon\nu\varepsilon\sigma\iota\alpha$) of the
earthly and heavenly world (Matt. 19:28), a restoration
($\alpha\pi\sigma\kappa\alpha\tau\alpha\sigma\tau\alpha\sigma\iota s$) of the lost (Acts 3: 21), a releasing of the
creature from the bondage of corruption (Rom. 8: 21), pre-
pared and assured by means of the resurrection and ascen-
sion of Jesus Christ to the right hand of God.

Further, while the rationalistic conception sees in the
serpent of Paradise only an emblem of wicked desire,[3] that
of the so-called mystic conception represents it as the instrument of Samael, i. e., the demoniac power of evil and
of death, and in this sense it is often said that through the
counsel of the serpent[4] man brought death upon himself,
and that death, even if not in that special case, yet in general is the result of sin.[5] Sin and death accordingly will
not cease till the head of the old serpent[6] is crushed, and
that is just what is hoped in the appearance of the Messiah,

---

1) ארם הראשין.   2) על ידי.

3) יצר הרע.

4) בעטיו של נחש.

5) אין מיתה בלא חטא.

6) נחש הקרמין.

as is paraphrased by the Jerusalem Targum (Gen. 3: 15 b);
"For them (mankind) there is no salvation, and for thee,
O serpent, there is no salvation; but they (mankind) will
one day attain comfort and restoration as far as the heel[1]
in the days of King Messiah." As the other Jerusalem
Targum shows, there lies at the bottom of this the thought
that the struggle going on through history between the
serpent and mankind is marked by a continual conquest and
yielding, a crushing of the head, i.e., a victory of those who
hold fast the law of God, and a bruising of the heel, and
thus a yielding of those who forsake God and His law. But
the coming of the Messiah determines the victory, and
brings healing even to the bruise upon the heel, which mankind has suffered from the serpent, while the serpent himself remains under the curse. At all events the Targum
says that the promise interwoven in the curse of the serpent will find its final fulfillment through the appearance
of the Messiah, and that is an agreement with Christianity
which cannot be too highly estimated.

The ancient synagogue also acknowledges the Messiah
as the Mediator of an eternal redemption. The Jerusalem
Targum, on Gen. 49: 18, designates the salvation upon
which the hope of the dying patriarch is fixed as the final,
eternal salvation, and paraphrases it in the following language: "Our father Jacob said, My soul waiteth not for
the redemption of Gideon, the son of Joash, for that is a
temporal redemption; and not for the redemption of Sam-
son, the son of Manoah, for that is a redemption which will
come to an end; but for the redemption which Thou hast
promised to bring to Thy people, the children of Israel,
through Thy Word,[2]—for this redemption my soul waiteth."
And there is added, "For Thy redemption is an eternal
redemption."[3] In another reading the passage signifies,
"No, but for the redemption of the Messiah, of the son of
David, who one day will redeem the children of Israel and

---

1) שׁיזייא בעקבא.

2) במימרך.

3) פורקן עלמין.

bring them back from exile,—for this redemption waiteth
my soul." According to one of these readings God accomplishes this enduring redemption through His Word,[1] who
is the means of His revelation in the world and in history;
and according to the other it is through the Messiah, the
son of David; that is, if we combine the two readings of
the personal human mediator of His revelation, in whom
involuntarily this thought forces itself upon us—His Word[2]
as it were, became flesh. We are very far from wishing to
attribute to Jewish declarations New Testament thoughts
in their apostolic sharpness and depth of meaning, but our
interest in the difference between the two is exceeded by
our interest in their relative agreement. In the statement
of ancient Jewish doctrine one may have as his object to
show how different its representatives are from Christian
ideas, even when they apparently agree. But it is much
more the object of the one who states Christian doctrine,
especially of one who would like to win Jews to Christianity, to show that the ancient Jewish theology (that is, that
theology which was not yet influenced by a tendency in
opposition to Christianity,) contains as an addition to the
Word of God in the Old Testament germs of thought,which
attain their development and their perfection in Christianity, or forms of thought which Christianity has filled with
a new and advanced contents given by revelation. Even
Ferdinand Weber, in his System of the Theology of the
Ancient Synagogue, translated by George Schnedermann
and myself (1880), has, in a one-sided manner, laid too much
stress on the differences. He says, for example, that the
theology of the ancient synagogue never connected the
Messiah and the essential Word of God[3] at the same time
referring to Isa. 9:6 and 7, where, as a seal of the prophecy
of the birth of the Messiah, it is stated, "The zeal of the
Lord of hosts will perform this." This is rendered by the
Targum, "Through the Word[4] of the Lord of hosts will

---

1) In the New Testament through His Λογος.

2) מימרא.

3) מימרא.

4) בממרא.

this be performed." But with a justice equal to that with which Weber refers to the difference between Jewish and Christian conceptions, and no less scientifically, we here affirm the resemblance of the one to the other. For as the Jewish theology, in addition to the Old Testament witnesses (*e. g.*, Psa. 33:6; 107:20), views the Word as the medium of power in the creation and government of the world, so does the Targum on Isa. 9:7 designate the coming of the Messiah into the world as the work of God through His Word, or what is the same thing, His *Logos.*

"The Word (ὁ Λογος) was made flesh," says John (1:14), and then continues, "and dwelt among us, . . . full of grace and truth." Without any doubt the apostle here means that in Jesus the Messiah, the divine Shechinah appeared in human form. For the ancient Jewish theology called the Shechinah[1] the dwelling of God, the presence, and especially the gracious presence of God among men. God Himself, as in His holiness, coming and dwelling here below with His own; as is said (*Aboth 3:3*), "When two sit together and discourse over the words of the law, there is the Shechinah present with them." And the ancient Jewish theology also affirms, as the end of human history, that God will again make His abode with men. "The Shechinah," says an old Midrash (*Tanchuma, 129 b*, Vienna edition), "dwelt originally here below, but after Adam's fall He withdrew farther and farther into heaven, and with Abraham began His gradual return." And another Midrash (*Pirke de Rabbi Eliezer, ch. 14*), says that the Holy Scripture speaks of ten descents[2] of God upon the earth, of which the tenth is to be expected at the last time. Does not this closely approach the thought that the appearance of the Messiah will be the deepest descent of God into human history? The Messianic names, "Immanuel," and the "Lord our Righteousness," confirm this. Only the name, "Mighty God"[3] (Isa. 9:6), which cannot, except with violence, be explained away,—*that only* passes the Jewish comprehension.

---

1) שׁכׅינה.

2) ירׅירׅית.

3) אל גבור.

We now put together a few witnesses in regard to the Messiah from the ancient synagogue, which agree with the Christian testimony, except that Christianity regards what was said of the Messiah as fulfilled in Jesus.

1. As Paul says of Christ (Col. 1:16), that God created all things through Him and for Him, so likewise in *Bereshith rabba*, ch. 2, Resh Lachish says of the Spirit which brooded over the waters of chaos, "This was the Spirit of King Messiah."[1]

2. As Paul (Gal. 6:2,) speaks of a law of Christ, and therefore of a Messianic law, whose commandments are summed up in the commandment of love, born of faith, so likewise we read in *Jalkut* on Isa., § 296, that the Holy One —Blessed be He!—intends through the Messiah to give a new law.[2]

3. As in Matt. 8:17, the confession of the 53d chapter of Isaiah, "Surely he hath borne our griefs and carried our sorrows," is mentioned as fulfilled in Jesus; so likewise in the Babylonian Talmud (*Sanhedrin 98 b,*) reference is made to the Messiah as taking human sorrows upon Himself in that He is considered as a sufferer, like Job and Rabbi Judah the Holy.

4. As Peter, in his first Epistle (1:19 ff), calls Christ the Lamb of God "fore-ordained before the foundation of the world," so likewise is it said (*Pesachim 54 a*) that the name of the Messiah was already made (came into existence,) before the world was made; and in *Pesikta Rabbathi* (Friedman's edition, p. 161,) it is said that He has taken vicarious suffering upon Himself since the six days of creation.[3]

5. John says in his first Epistle (2:1 ff), "We have an Advocate with the Father, Jesus Christ the righteous; and He is the propitiation for our sins, and not for ours only, but also for the sins of the whole world." And in *Jalkut* on Isaiah, § 359, the Messiah promises to complete the work of redemption destined to Him from the beginning, when

1) דא רוחא דמלכא משיחא.
2) תורה חדשת.
3) מששת ימי בראשית.

He says: "O Lord of the world, with inward exulting joy
I take it upon myself on condition that no one of Israel
shall be lost, and that not alone those who live in my
days shall have salvation, but also those who lie in the dust
of the grave; and that not alone those who die in my days
shall have salvation, but also those dead who have died
from the days of the first Adam till now, and that not
these only, but also that those dead-born in my days shall
have salvation; and not the dead-born alone, but also all
those whom Thou hast in mind to call into being, and those
not yet come into being. I will enter immediately into the
agreement and will take it immediately upon myself."

6. In the first Epistle of Peter (3: 18 ff), it is affirmed
that Christ, "being put to death in the flesh, but quickened
by the Spirit," went in the Spirit "and preached unto the
spirits in prison;" and similar to this is what is affirmed in
Jalkut on Isaiah, § 296, that the son of David will pray for
the dwellers in the underworld, and that the wicked who
say Amen to this prayer will by this one Amen be saved
from hell.

7. The Epistle to the Hebrews shows that Christ, as
the antitype of Melchizedek, is far above Abraham (7: 4),
higher than Moses (3: 3), higher than the angels (1: 4), and
exactly after this manner is Isa 52: 13, explained in *Jalkut*,
§ 238: "King Messiah will be higher than Abraham, and
lifted up above Moses, and will stand far higher than the
ministering angels.

8. In Hebrews 1: 13 the question is asked, "To which
of the angels said he at any time, Sit on my right hand?"
And in *Jalkut* on the Psalms, § 869, we find among many
mistaken interpretations, the New Testament thought:
"One day the Holy One—Blessed be He—will call King
Messiah to sit at His right hand." So also Rabbi Akiba
understands the 110th Psalm (*Chagiga 14 1*), though Rabbi
Joseph the Galilean, objects to this and finds in the throne
of the Messiah at the right hand of God a profanation of
the Shechinah.

9. To the question of the high priest (Mark 14: 61, 62),
"Art thou the Christ, the Son of the Blessed?" Jesus said,

" I am; and ye shall see the Son of man sitting on the right
hand of power, and coming in the clouds of heaven." Also
the Talmud (*Sanhedrin* 98 a) presupposes the Messianic
reference of Daniel 7: 13: He it is who shall appear in the
clouds of heaven, or riding upon an ass; and the Targum
on 1 Chron. 34, remarks upon the name Anani,[1] "That is
the King Messiah, who shall one day be revealed."

10. And as Jesus declares (John 5: 25), "Verily, verily,
I say unto you, the hour is coming, and now is, when the
dead shall hear the voice of the Son of God; and they that
hear shall live." So likewise, according to Sanhedrin 98 b,
the Messiah is called ינון and that too—as this symbolic
name is explained in *Pirke de Eliezer*, ch. 32, and elsewhere,
—as He who makes those who sleep in the dust of the
grave to germinate, that is, who awakens them to new life.

· "But," some one will perhaps object, "to put together
these passages gives a false impression, for they are witnesses from different times and different books." As though
we did not know that! But they all belong to the Talmudic
period, or at least to the Talmudic literature;[3] and they all
belong to the time after Christ, which, far from weakening
the force of this testimony, only strengthens it in a manner
astonishing and even startling. The second possible objec-
tion is that "what is there said is not the confession of the
whole synagogue, but of single individuals." But these individuals are men whose authority is of the greatest weight,
like Resh Lachish and Rabbi Akiba, and when the same
declarations are found in the Targum they appear as in a
certain measure accepted by the consciousness of the people, or at least there is a decided tendency towards such an
acceptance. And in the third place one may endeavor to
resist the impression of these evidences by bringing up
these points in which they differ from the Christian state-
ments. But what we wish to show remains unmoved, and
is not weakened by any of these objections. For in any
case this shows that the fundamental ideas of Christianity

Cloud man. ענני (1
2) Jinnon, Psa. 72: 17.
3) We have intentionally omitted references to the *Sohar Literature*.

have their roots in Judaism, in ancient Judaism, and not in
that Judaism which later let go its hold of the prophetic
Word; and they likewise show that Christianity does not by
any means force upon Judaism new and foreign ideas which
it might not thoroughly assimilate if it only would. The
fundamental question is, and ever remains the question,
" Is Jesus the Messiah, or shall we expect another?"

Let us look, for example, for a moment at the Targum
on Isa. 52: 13; 53. It begins (52: 13), "Behold, my servant,
the Messiah, shall do wondrous things." This personal
conception of the Servant of the Lord is not retained in
the course of the translation; the collective idea of Israel
enduring judgment gains finally the upper hand and the
representation becomes gradually secular and warlike. But
for our purpose it will suffice to refer to ch. 53: 4, 5, where
the Targum translates, " He [the Messiah,] will make in-
tercession for our sins, and for His sake our misdeeds will
be forgiven, while we thought Him scourged, smitten of
the Lord, and loaded with afflictions, and He will build the
temple which was profaned by our sins, which was dis-
honored by our misdeeds, and by His teaching will great
peace come to us, and if we hear His words our sins will
be forgiven." The translation contains unjustifiable alter-
ations, but in spite of them the thought remains, which is
indeed the fundamental thought of Christianity, that
through the merits, through the word, through the inter-
cession of the Messiah forgiveness of sins will be wrought.
If then, the Jew recognizes in Jesus the Messiah, it is only
the Messianic hopes of the ancient synagogue which he
sees realized in Him. In accordance with these he may
confess: " He has sacrificed Himself for us, He has proclaimed to us the way of salvation, and He appears before
God as a high priest in our behalf."

There remains now but one more important point in
which the Jewish Messianic idea and the Christian conception of Christ agree, one indeed little considered, and
yet very significant, and which cannot be gainsaid.

THE Messianic hope, as it is voiced in the Jewish literature before and after Christ, exhibits different forms. It is now more earthly, national and warlike; now more mystical, universal, and ethico-religious. But there is one fundamental trait common to all the Messianic conceptions; that is, the son of David, who does not transfer His dominion to a bodily successor. He is not a king, like the kings of this earth, in whose stead at death there succeeds a son as heir to the throne. He exists in no marriage relation from which spring bodily children. Furthermore, there is a singlar representation according to which the one Messiah is made into two; a Messiah the son of Joseph, who was against the world-power, and a Messiah the son of David, who accomplished the victory over the world-power. Now these both are childless, they have no sons in whom their life and work are continued. The Messiah, the son of David, is not the founder of a dynasty. He is the sole occupant of the throne, without a change. He reigns eternally. If, however, a limited continuance be ascribed to the dominion of the Messiah, then there must be intended a period of time passing over into eternity. For the days of the Messiah[1] belong to the future world;[2] they form the transition from the temporal form of the present to the eternal form of the hereafter.

Marriage is a divinely ordered institution. Without it the human race cannot be perpetuated, that is, in families. Therefore, especially according to the Jewish idea, marriage is the duty of a man. But to think of the Messiah in the married state does not simply contradict a cabalistic exaggeration.[3] The Messiah is unmarried, as imagined and represented in Jewish literature both before and after Christ. And this is scriptural. For as the prophetic word speaks of the ancestors (fathers) of the Messiah, but not of a bodily father, only of his bodily mother (Isa. 7: 14, Micah 5: 2, Jer. 31: 32, cf. Isa. 49: 1), so also it never speaks of a spouse of the King Messiah. Whenever there is a refer-

---

(1 ימות המשית.   2) העילם הבא.

3) Shabbathai Zebi married Sara, the beautiful Pole, who threw herself upon his neck as the destined wife of the Messiah, but the glory of the false Messiah was by no means enhanced thereby.

ence to a relation between the Messiah and a wife, this
wife is the church, the antitype of the Shulamite; and
whenever there is a reference to the children of the Messiah, it is his people who are meant, whose Eternal Father[1] He is, the holy seed of those redeemed by Him. Isa. 6:
13; 53:10. In the passage, Psa. 45:16 (Hebrew Bible v. 17),
"Instead of thy fathers shall be thy children," the Targum,
interpreting the psalm Messianically, renders בנך צדיקיא. (thy
children, the righteous). For marriage, although a divine
institution, is, nevertheless, only an earthly and temporal
relation, while the Messiah is a personality lifted far above
earthly conditions.   His feet rest on the earth, but His
head towers above the heavens.

Just for this reason is the government and kingdom
of the Messiah always designated by the prophets as eternal. The Messiah himself is an eternal king, without a
successor. Isa. 9:7, Ezek. 37:25. And it is simply impossible that the Messiah should be meant by that prince in
Ezek. ch. 40–48, who leaves princely dignity and domain to
his children. The Targum deliberately translates נשיא[2]
in this concluding vision of Ezekiel by רבא,[3] but where the
Messiah is foretold by a prophet as the second David (Ezek.
34:24; 37:25), it renders the same word מלכא.[4] It is a much
more self-consistent thought which the people expressed
when they failed to understand Jesus' prophecy of His ap-
proaching death: "We have heard out of the law that
Christ abideth forever."   And so also we read in the proclamation of the birth of Jesus (Luke 1:32, 33): "The Lord
God shall give unto him the throne of his father David;
and he shall reign over the house of Jacob forever, and of
his kingdom there shall be no end."

Judaism and Christianity therefore agree in this, that
the Messiah is a personality, absolute and eternal, lifted far
above earthly family life and far above every earthly lim-

1) אבי־עד.

2) The Prince.
3) Great One.
4) King.

itation. And in this all that bear the name of Christian
are as one. To be sure, there is just now in vogue in the
Christian world a theology which affords to Judaism weap-
ons both offensive and defensive against the doctrine of
the church and against the historical character of our religious documents; but we may, nevertheless, comfort ourselves in the midst of all this confusion, sure that this as-
sistance will not suffice for the justification of Judaism.
For in Christianity one may occupy the unitarian, the trin-
itarian, the rationalistic, or the supernatural stand-point,
but it always will remain that Christianity is the religion
of completed ethics, and that Jesus is the great, holy, and
divine Man, whose appearance on earth divides the history
of the world. And we may regard the mystery of the
atonement as we will, it will, nevertheless, always remain
that the blood of this Jesus, who is the antitype of Abel,
the slain innocent, speaketh better things than that of
Abel, since it asks not vengeance, but favor, for the guilty.

There has recently appeared a publication bearing the
title, "Undogmatic Christianity." In this the question is
raised in reference to the gospel critics, how anything
which is the subject and product of scientific inquiry can be
the foundation of an assured religious faith. The answer is,
that this consideration disappears if we withdraw into the
innermost depths of the holy character of Christ, "who is
far above all the fluctuations of theology and historical
science, just as a lofty mountain peak lifts itself above the
clouds. For has it ever been doubted that He was uncon-
ditionally obedient to His heavenly Father, He who, loving His brethren with an undying love, was faithful even
unto death, He who, never moved by temptation and never
embittered by ingratitude, was incomparable in the fear-
less truthfulness of His soul, and in His gentle meekness,
He who was led patient as a lamb to the slaughter praying
for His murderers? Therefore from the time of His sojourn upon earth to the present day, He has won mankind,
has conquered their most stubborn resistance, and has led
them in countless numbers to God. This character, wondrous in its simplicity, influences us all, whether condemn-

ing or inspiring us. He accompanies us in all relations of
life, and in all conditions of feeling, as the pole-star the
nightly wanderer. No one into whose consciousness He
once has come is free as before. The Christ who accomplishes this down to the present day, and to all eternity,
we must call the historic Christ, for he calls forth again
and again the mightiest historical forces."

This is true, but the historic forces go yet deeper. He
is surely the living ideal of noble humanity which has ris-
en upon men and has poured His light and warmth upon
them. But He is more than that; He is the Christ, the goal
of the words and ways of God in the Old Testament. He
is the Mediator between God and man, between Israelite
and Gentile, between heaven and earth, and between time
and eternity. Having passed through death into glory,
He has laid the foundation of the kingdom of God, the
completion of which is assured because thus laid. When
once Israel shall greet him with a better Hosanna than the
first,[1] then, and not till then, will the consummation of this
divine kingdom draw near.

"God hath concluded them all in unbelief," says the
apostle in reference to Israel, "that He might have mercy
upon all." Rom. 11: 32. Brethren of the house of Israel!
at last now break through the ban of unbelief, ere mercy
shall have run her course.

---

1) Matt. 23: 39.

THE END

CORRIGENDA.

עֵדוּת לְיִשְׂרָאֵל

"EDUTH LE ISRAEL,"

(Witness to Israel,)

A Hebrew monthly devoted to the furtherance of mo:al
and religious life amongst the Jews.

EDITOR,

——M. LOEWEN,——

Kampiana Street 3.   Lemberg, Galizier.

THE PECULIAR PEOPLE,

A CHRISTIAN MONTHLY,

DEVOTED TO JEWISH INTERESTS.

EDITOR,

THE REV. WILLIAM C. DALAND,

LEONARDSVILLE, N. Y.

Published by the American Sabbath Tract Society, Alfred Centre, New York.

www.ingramcontent.com/pod-product-compliance
Lightning Source LLC
Chambersburg PA
CBHW022021080426
42733CB00007B/676